INTO HIS PRESENCE

INTO HIS PRESENCE

The Education Department is
grateful to Mr. Terry Treman of
Grand Rapids, Michigan, for his
photography that appears on the
cover and in the text.

Library of Congress Cataloging in Publication Data

De Jong, James A., 1941-
    Into his presence.

    1. Reformed Church—Liturgy.   2. Christian Reformed
Church—Liturgy.   I. Title.
BX9427.D45   1985   264'.05731   84-28576
ISBN 0-933140-99-1

ISBN 0-933140-99-1

CONTENTS

To come "into his [God's] presence" is the psalmist's description of worship (Ps. 95:2). That phrase is a fitting title for a book that defines worship as "a prescribed, corporate meeting between God and his people" in which God is praised and the people are blessed. Though the psalmist's phrase is more poetic than the definition, the same sense of wonder and awe at the privilege of appearing before the Lord permeates both the psalm and this book.

This book is designed as part of a course. Read separately it can be a valuable guide to the principles and practice of worship in the Reformed tradition. Studied with others in a class setting, it can be a means to evaluate and renew a congregation's worship patterns.

This course is designed as part of a church school curriculum called BIBLE WAY. This curriculum is a Reformed attempt at developing comprehensive church education materials that are both biblical and confessional, both evangelistic and covenantal, both for children and for adults. *Into His Presence*, one of the offerings for adults, teaches about the church, its history, its structure, and its practices.

The author of this book, Dr. James A. De Jong, helped also to design the course. As a former chairperson of the Liturgical Committee of the Christian Reformed Church, for many years he served the church with advice and guidance in this area of its life. As a former professor at Dordt College, he taught students the more theoretical aspects of worship. As the current president of Calvin Seminary, he now guides and teaches future pastors who will be leading in worship. So he is triply qualified to serve as author of this study.

The other elements of this course, the study guides called Postscript (included in the textbook) and the leader's guide, were prepared by the Education Department staff with numerous suggestions from Dr. De Jong.

We offer this material with the hope and prayer that it may serve to deepen both your understanding and experience of the worship of our God.

Harvey A. Smit

My intent in writing this book is to help Reformed people think through their worship.

Thinking through the worship we collectively give God is important today. The Christian church is in the middle of liturgical reevaluation and renewal. Fresh approaches, new musical and liturgical resources, a deep desire for genuineness and participation are all features of the present worship scene. In this terrain it is imperative to get our biblical and theological bearings. We badly need liturgical discrimination. Equally as important, we must be delivered from liturgical hangups and phobias. The ten following chapters are a modest attempt to meet both needs by working through some basic ideas about worship.

Deliberately, then, these materials are not a worship handbook or even worship resources. Resourceful people, however, will see many connections between what is contained here and the services in their churches. Those who read and discuss these pages will be inclined to scrutinize, reaffirm, or modify the worship in their church. Most importantly, the book should make what we do in worship more gratifying to God and more meaningful for us.

Of course, these reflections are not final thoughts. Initiated in seminary training, stimulated on a denominational committee, refined through reading and by students in a liturgy course, they will continue to develop. I am grateful to the Christian Reformed Board of Publications, which has judged them to be sufficiently useful to the church to warrant production.

James A. De Jong

DEFINING REFORMED WORSHIP

THE URGE TO WORSHIP, TO APPEASE, to adore, to depend on forces greater than human has fostered a baffling variety of religions in the world. Each has customs of worship which often raises questions for the "outsider": Why did the Ammonites incinerate their firstborn sons on Molech's altar? Why do Moslems abstain from food during daylight hours of Ramadan? Why would a devout Hindu businessman forsake his livelihood and family to become an ascetic wandering holy man? How can university-educated North Americans trade their upward mobility for life in an Oregon ashram? What compels people to consult the stars, to venerate the memory of ancestors, to cover their mouths and noses with gauze so as not to inhale and kill an insect, or to sacrifice a dog in the woods by the light of a full moon?

In answer to such questions the council leaders at Vatican II expressed a line of Roman Catholic thinking centuries old:

> From ancient times down to the present, there has existed among diverse peoples a certain perception of that hidden power which hovers over the course of things and over the events of human life; at times, indeed, recognition can be found of a Supreme Divinity and of a Supreme Father too. Such a perception and such

a recognition instill the lives of these peoples with a profound religious sense.

—"Declaration on the Relationship of the Church to Non-Christian Religions," *The Documents of Vatican II*

John Calvin expressed similar views. Everyone, he said, has "a sense of divinity." This becomes the "seed of religion" that flowers into an exotic variety of human worship. But, Calvin warned, these variations are really mutations. They compound our human, sinful inability to know God completely or to perceive him clearly. Only in Jesus Christ can our spiritual blindness be healed, our blurred vision corrected, and our worship made acceptable. Worship in the name of Christ and according to Scripture's directive is the only true worship. All other forms, said Calvin, are false.

Roman Catholic and Protestant thinkers, then, have a similar explanation for worship outside the Christian faith. They agree that people are created with an innate drive to worship—to recognize, to consult, to fear, and even to compliment forces and persons greater than themselves. The wild, contradictory diversity of human worship reflects the cultural, the intellectual, and above all the religious meanderings of the human spirit. Through the centuries it has reached no agreement on how or whom to worship.

THE COMMONNESS IN CHRISTIAN WORSHIP

In contrast, all Christian worship seems to have a basic cohesion. What holds it together is not so much a common structure as the only name through which God accepts worship. The Lord Jesus Christ is the common mediator through whom all Christians worship God. Worship flows from Christ's new community, the church, through the channel of Jesus' name, to God. God accepts the church's worship for the sake of Jesus' name.

A second factor holding all Christian worship together is the Scriptures. The Bible contributes to all Christian traditions that which is common and basic in their worship. It teaches us both the spirit and the content of true prayer. The Bible indicts sinners and consoles penitents, thus sug-

gesting the pattern for confession and forgiveness in Christian worship. The Bible, in the Psalms and in Revelation, shows us how to praise God. The Bible commands us to listen to God's preachers, to baptize new believers into the community, and to fellowship around the Lord's table. All styles of Christian worship include these elements. So the Bible and the name of Christ create a basic unity in Christian worship.

THE DIFFERENCES IN CHRISTIAN WORSHIP

Differences in worship from one Christian group to another are obvious. The basic unity is camouflaged by a wide range of styles, rituals, and emphases.

Some of these differences are theologically based. Consider the role of the Holy Spirit in worship. Quakers stress that the Spirit is given to the entire community and moves freely among believers to give counsel, insight, and inspiration. Accordingly, Quakers sit quietly in the meeting house, waiting for the Spirit's coming. Whoever receives the Spirit's inner light or constraint rises to edify the congregation. By contrast most mainline Protestant denominations stress the Spirit's work through the Word. Spirit-led leaders, after years of study, are called and ordained to preach to the body of believers the divine truth of the Word. Thus a different theology of the Holy Spirit produces a different style of worship.

Other differences reflect cultural tastes. While African Christians worship God to the beat of a drum, Christians in the European tradition prefer the solemn sounds of the pipe organ. And while some Christians enjoy the subtly subjective, experiential hymns produced by nineteenth-century romanticism, others insist on hymns that speak not of our feelings, but more traditionally and biblically of the faithfulness and majesty of God ("A Mighty Fortress Is Our God"). Christians in the Eastern Orthodox Church, for example, prefer worship marked with formality, tradition, and mystery. In contrast, the informality of American frontier religion endures in the sawdust trail of Baptist revival meetings.

Some of the sharpest differences in worship come from confessions and creeds.

The Protestant view of Christ's atoning death as a completed sacrifice is reflected in their celebration of the Lord's Supper. The Roman Catholic view of the mass as the grace-conferring actual body and blood of the Lord produces a very different sacrament.

Some churches, convinced that only what Scripture commands ought to be included in Christian worship, are liturgically austere and simple. Others, depending on ancient, subtle nuances given to biblical words and symbols, have a ritual richness.

Christian worship, then, is both unified and diverse. Both characteristics are important. The one makes possible genuine ecumenical praise. The other defines, far more than is commonly realized, who and what we are as Christians. Genuine worship will always be focused by cultural, theological, and historical considerations. That's part of our creatureliness. But true worship also belongs to the great euphony of angels, humans, and the rest of creation praising God together. Through Jesus Christ our limited worship becomes part of the limitless adoration of God which will fill the new heavens and the new earth.

REFORMED WORSHIP

This book unapologetically looks at worship from a Reformed angle. It is written to help Reformed Christians better understand what occurs in their worship. Worshiping God enthusiastically, in the richness of their own tradition, Reformed believers, like the altos blending their tones in a choir, contribute significantly to the overall praise of God.

Included in the Reformed tradition are the Presbyterian and Congregational churches which began in Britain and those churches which spring from parallel "Reformed" movements on the European continent. A theological and a confessional compatibility, rooted historically in John Calvin, binds these groups together. Two early, important examples of Reformed worship are Calvin's "The Form of Church Prayers" (1542) and "The Westminister Directory of Public Worship" (1644).

Reformed worship may be defined simply as "a prescribed, corporate meeting between God and his people, in which God is praised and his church is blessed." Explaining this definition piece by piece should help us better to understand our Reformed worship.

WORSHIP IS A MEETING

As a meeting, worship is distinct from meditation, contemplation, and other private, reflective, spiritual activities. A believer may muse on a sinful act and the pain it causes others, or ponder the mystery of God's sacrifice on the cross. But in such preoccupations, he or she is not addressing God.

14 Meditation may be a high religious art. But while important in the Christian faith, it is surpassed by worship. Worship is a face-to-face meeting and exchange. When Christian worship is so trivial, so novel, so cluttered, so mechanical, or so traditional that it lacks any awareness of meeting with God, it has failed the first and basic test of true worship.

All of life is either an obedient or a disobedient response to God. Reformed thinkers have often emphasized the need for a worshipful attitude throughout the believer's existence. Such general, comprehensive worship is the context of worship as a meeting, but the two are not identical. Worship as a meeting is a conscious, deliberate, and explicit encounter with God. Like a business luncheon or committee meeting, it is scheduled into the rhythm of our lives.

WORSHIP IS A CORPORATE MEETING

Individual, private, devotional exercises are a kind of worship vital to our spiritual well-being. They ought to be daily events in a believer's life. Such devotions should include both the opportunity for God to address us in his Word and for us to address God in prayer. But personal devotions are not corporate worship.

Even family devotions, worship with a group of friends, and chapel exercises are not, strictly speaking, corporate worship. For while these bodies of people may be intimately and organically bound together, they lack the universal, comprehensive character of the church as the office-led body of Christ. Our definition of worship as a corporate meeting refers precisely to the officially called and supervised worship of the one, holy, catholic, and apostolic church. These four adjectives can, in a sense, be applied to other Christian groups, but they are usually reserved for the organized, instituted congregation of believers. We mean by worship, therefore, the worship of the church on the corner of Fourth and Main. We are talking about worship in church!

WORSHIP IS A PRESCRIBED, CORPORATE MEETING

Prescribed means not that worship occurs at a designated time and place or by the command of Jesus Christ, although these are significant dimensions of worship. It means that worship follows a prescribed order or format with prescribed components. This order is commonly called the liturgy.

A liturgy is like a recipe. Every good cook has a favorite recipe that makes her potato salad unique. Similarly, each church has its own liturgy. The variation between the liturgy of churches within the same denomination may be minute; between widely separate traditions, immense.

It is essential that liturgy serve worship. It should be a vehicle to enable worship, not impede it. A good understanding of the history of the liturgy and of the rationale for its components will enhance worship. It may even help improve the liturgy for the sake of better worship. While liturgy and worship are distinguishable, they are never separable.

WORSHIP IS A PRESCRIBED, CORPORATE MEETING BETWEEN GOD AND HIS PEOPLE

Worship is often characterized as a dialogue. In any liturgy there are places where God speaks and other places where the people respond. There are several exchanges between God and the worshipers.

Yet the idea of dialogue has certain deficiencies. Dialogue is usually between equals. In worship God convenes the meeting and remains in charge through his appointed delegates. Like in-

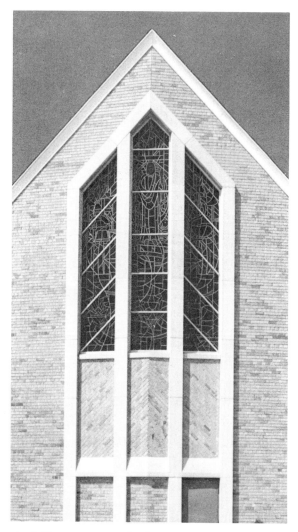

first of all with God. Our sense of oneness comes from our common address to God. We speak to him in unison. He addresses us as his church. Worship that directs attention on individual members risks becoming banter with and about people. Meeting with each other may be enjoyable, informative, even uplifting, but it is not worship.

Defined as a meeting between God and his people, worship is necessarily restricted. It is not for everyone. It is for the community that knows God by faith and approaches him through Jesus its Lord. "His people" refers not to all humans—his by virtue of creation, but to the body of believers—his through re-creation by water and the Word.

Thus, when some people, say, "I would never take anyone to our church in order to interest them in the Christian faith," they may be right! Interesting people in the faith is not the task of worship but of Christians equipped through worship. Worship is not designed to win converts, but to strengthen the converted. In daily contacts with others Christians witness and evangelize. On Sunday Christians approach God as the body of believers. This is not meant to disparage evangelistic preaching, just to distinguish it carefully from liturgical preaching. Like Peter and Paul, the Wesleys and Whitefield, modern evangelists should preach in shopping malls, parks, beaches, and neighborhoods. But in worship God meets his people.

A very important, often overlooked, implication of this definition is that worship must be meaningful for children. As members of the church by virtue of God's covenant confirmed in their baptism, children are God's little people. They, as well as adults, must be participants in worship.

WORSHIP IS A MEETING IN WHICH GOD IS PRAISED

Praise is the central intent and dominant tone of worship. The Psalms use this term *praise* as the

vited dinner guests, God's people attend worship by divine invitation. Dialogue may ramble. Worship does not; its exchanges are prescribed.

The interaction occurs primarily between God and his people as a group. While aware of each other, Christians do not worship to visit with one another. They remember Suzie's broken leg and John and Sally's wedding in prayer, but they address God, not each other. Worship's fellowship is basic word to characterize worship. And then the Psalms, and other Scriptures bid us to glorify, magnify, extol, adore, rejoice before, bless, sing hallelujah to, and make a joyful noise to the Lord. These words all capture the exuberance with which the worshipers praise God for his greatness and goodness.

But praise can be stretched to include also the reverence, the awe, the holy fear the worshiper feels; the contrition, the penitence, the confession of sin, the appeal for forgiveness the worshiper brings; and the thanks, the gratitude, the dependence the believers show to God. All these aspects of the worship service are different forms our praise takes.

Worship Is a Meeting in Which the Church Is Blessed

Not only do people give in worship, they also receive. God's blessing, given to his people, is the effect which worship has on the church.

The Word of God is the source of blessing in the service. According to one expert on Reformed worship, this occurs at four points. First, God speaks his Word of greeting at the beginning of the service—he reassures the congregation of his presence in their lives. God's second Word is a word of forgiveness following the confession of sin—he blesses the church with pardon and reconciliation. Third, God speaks his Word of instruction—reassurance, understanding, instruction, correction, inspiration, and guidance are all forms of God's blessing in the sermon. At the close of worship God speaks his fourth Word, the Word of benediction—he blesses his people with the promise of well-being through the week.

Even in the parts of the liturgy in which the people address God, they are blessed. Like the genuine giving of a birthday present, the believer finds that in worship also, "it is more blessed to give than to receive" (Acts 20:35).

True worship then, in all its parts just described, is the church's coming "into his presence."

A. PERSONAL QUESTIONS/COMMENTS ON CHAPTER 1

B. Discussion Starters:
Agree/Disagree Statements

Please indicate the extent to which you agree or disagree with each of the statements below, keeping in mind chapter 1's definition of Reformed worship. The point of the exercise is to apply that definition and to sample various opinions from the class, not to arrive at consensus or resolution!

Statement 1 I'm in favor of more congregational participation in the service. Too much of the burden is on the pastor. It seems to me we could do more with our responses, maybe using some litanies or chants once in a while. Members of the congregation could read Scripture or give short testimonies. Women with musical gifts could lead some singing (men most often get that job). Children could come forward and gather around the pulpit to hear a children's sermon delivered by a good storyteller from the congregation. They should also be able to join the congregation in singing at least one children's song per service. Except for choirs and special music, we tend to leave too much to the minister and too little to the congregation.

Strongly Agree	Agree	Uncertain	Disagree	Strongly Disagree
(1)	*(2)*	*(3)*	*(4)*	*(5)*

Statement 2 I think worship services should include a strong element of fellowship with fellow believers as well as with God. Otherwise, why not worship alone at home instead of with the body of Christ, the church? We are one in the Lord, and I think our oneness is helped by chanting "good morning" to the pastor, by shaking hands with our neighbors at the beginning of the service, by hearing reports about the sick or, yes, even about upcoming social events like picnics and ballgames. I feel closer to fellow members when we do things like share a favorite text, pass the peace, or even (occasionally) hold hands during prayer. Isn't one of the purposes of the sacrament of communion to strengthen our fellowship with each other as well as with God? So I say, come to church to worship God *and* to have fellowship with each other.

Strongly Agree	Agree	Uncertain	Disagree	Strongly Disagree
(1)	*(2)*	*(3)*	*(4)*	*(5)*

Statement 3 "Worship is not for everyone. It is for the community which knows God by faith and approaches him through Jesus its Lord. . . . Interesting people in the faith is not the task of worship but of Christians equipped through worship. Worship is not designed to win converts, but to strengthen the converted. In daily contacts with others, Christians witness and evangelize. On Sunday, Christians approach God as the body of believers" (from chapter 1).

Strongly Agree	Agree	Uncertain	Disagree	Strongly Disagree
(1)	*(2)*	*(3)*	*(4)*	*(5)*

C. Recipes for Reformed Worship

Compare *one* of the two "recipes for Reformed worship" (page 19) with the liturgy your congregation uses. Some discussion questions follow:

1. What basic differences do you see?

2. Read the second paragraph from the end of chapter 1; then locate the "four Words" (greeting, forgiveness, instruction, benediction) in each liturgy.

3. Give an example of dialogue in each liturgy.

4. How do the two liturgies differ from non-Reformed worship?

Two Recipes for Reformed Worship

Calvin's "Form of Prayers," 1542	*Westminster Directory, 1644*
"Our help is in the name of the Lord, who made heaven and earth. Amen"	Call to worship
Short call to confession, followed by prayer of confession	Prayer asking for God's holy presence, acceptance of the worshipers, and blessing on the readings of the Word
Singing of a metrical psalm	Old Testament reading
Prayer for illumination	New Testament reading
Scripture lesson	Singing of a metrical psalm
Sermon	Prayer of confession, intercession, and illumination
Intercessory prayer, concluded with paraphrase of Lord's Prayer	Sermon
* * * * *	Prayer of thanksgiving and intercession
Appended prayer for proper celebration of the supper	Lord's Prayer
Apostles Creed	* * * * *
Words of institution, 1 Corinthians 11:23–29	Exhortation and Invitation
Set form of exhortation, including the *sursum corda*	Consecration of the elements
The communion, during which Scripture was read and/or appropriate psalms were sung	Words of institution, from the Gospels or 1 Corinthians 11:23–27
Prayer of thanksgiving	Prayer of consecration, including the *epiclesis*
* * * * *	Fraction, distribution, and communion
Aaronic benediction, Numbers 6:24–25	Exhortation
(Items between the asterisks were included at communion services	Prayer of thanksgiving
	* * * * *
	Singing of a metrical psalm
	Benediction

Explanation of Communion Terms

Su sum corda—the instruction, dating from the third century, to "lift your hearts to the Lord."

Epiclesis—prayer for the presence of the Holy Spirit, a practice dating from the early church.

Fraction—the ancient practice of breaking the bread.

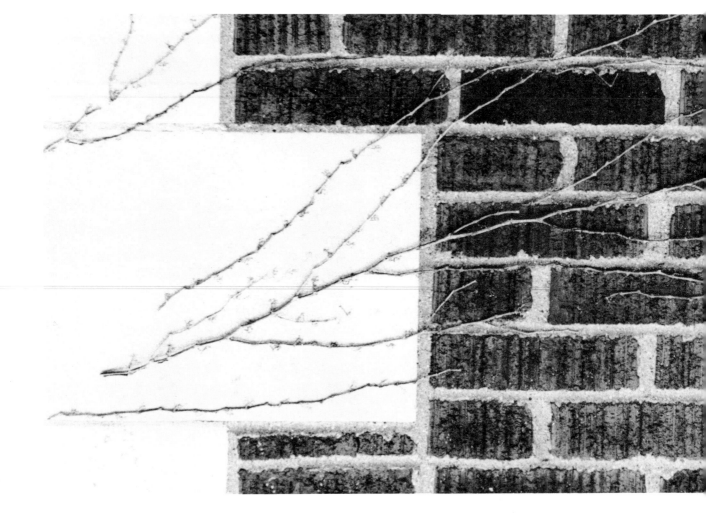

ROOTS OF REFORMED WORSHIP

T HE VISITOR PAUSED FOR A MOMENT in the narthex of a crowded European sanctuary. Spotting a gap in a rear pew, he slid into it. The service was about to begin, and the visitor, worried that his limited knowledge of the language and the liturgy would make him conspicuous, decided to follow the lead of the austere-looking man seated next to him. A few minutes later, as the minister and elders entered, the man beside him arose. So did the visitor. So did twenty-five to thirty other men. But the rest of the congregation—about a thousand people in all—remained seated. The blushing visitor quickly sat down, positive all eyes in the building were indicting him for his presumptuous, irreverent behavior.

Most of us who have worshiped in an unfamiliar church know how the visitor felt. A strange pattern of worship often makes us liturgically clumsy. We stand when the congregation kneels. We feel conspicuous paging through a worship book that skips erratically from one section to another. The clergy's garb and gestures, the smells and sounds of worship are unfamiliar and uncomfortable to us. And progressing step-by-step through the service becomes an ordeal.

Fortunately, in spite of the strangeness, most services share common elements. A person who knows a little about the form of Christian worship generally can anticipate what is coming next. That happens because most liturgies have been shaped to some degree by Old Testament religion. The differences between them—like the standing men our visitor joined—come from embellishments people have made throughout the Christian centuries. But their roots are the same.

OLD TESTAMENT WORSHIP

Worship began in the family. And many of the elements present in that early family worship are still part of our worship today. When Noah left the ark, he expressed his grateful devotion to God through a burnt offering which smelled good in the Lord's nose (Gen. 8:20–22). We fill collection plates to say thank you to God, but our spirit is the same as Noah's. In fact, all the patriarchs worshiped in ways that are familiar to us. Abram lit an offering of dedication and called on God's name (Gen. 12:7–8). Abraham's servant knelt and worshiped God for his steadfast love (Gen. 24:26-27). Isaac meditated (Gen. 24:63). And Jacob tithed (Gen. 28:18–22).

The important point is that worship in early Genesis was patriarchal. The father and leader of the tribe was also the priest and religious instructor. The Bible never retracts this emphasis on the family altar. Even after Moses established a complicated system of corporate worship, parents were commanded to give their children daily religious instruction (Deut. 6:13). Wise fathers guided their children to honor God (Prov. 3:1–2, 9–10; Eph. 6:4). And wise children benefited from that training (2 Tim. 3:15). It is apparent throughout the Bible that God's people value family worship.

At Mt. Sinai Moses introduced corporate, organized worship—a worship built around the first table of the Ten Commandments. The following breakdown tells us something about the spirit of Mosaic worship.

Even though Christians today are still bound by the first table of the Law, most of us would feel out of place in the Old Testament tabernacle or temple. We'd be repulsed if our minister slit a bull's throat at the door of our church, collected a basin of its blood, and poured or wiped it on walls, floors, and furniture in the church. We would be appalled if he carefully trimmed the fat from the animal's entrails, then laid it in a hot fire where we could hear it sputter and sizzle, and later burned the rest of the carcass in the town dump. Yet those are exactly the things Moses stipulated for a sin offering (Lev. 4:1-12).

Christ paid the high price for our repulsion through his once-for-all sacrifice for our sins. It, too, was a bloody, life-giving appeasement of God's just anger. But because it was the perfect, heavenly version of the Old Testament copies, it put an end to ritual, sacrificial bloodshed (Heb. 9:15–28). We no longer need to sacrifice animals as part of worship, but we should not be deluded into thinking all is well. Sin saps life. Its wages is death. And our worship, like that of Moses, must recognize that our health and life were purchased

Commandment	Content	Application to Worship
First	No gods before Yahweh	The *Person* to be Worshiped
Second	No images or other creaturely likenesses	The *Manner* of Worship
Third	Honor God's person by esteeming his name.	The *Spirit* of Worship
Fourth	Keep the Sabbath Day holy.	The *Time* of Worship

by the life of Another who died in our place.

Other Old Testament offerings also have their New Testament counterparts. And although most of us would be uncomfortable at any of those Old Testament ceremonies, we would recognize familiar motifs in them. The burnt offering (Lev. 1) conveyed devotion and heart commitment, now offered spiritually in Christian worship services. The cereal offering (Lev. 2) expressed thanks, now shown with money or articulated in our prayers. The peace offering (Lev. 3) maintained the reconciled harmony with God and others, a harmony which we now foster through Christian fellowship. The tithes of produce and flocks (Lev. 27:30-32) are now paid by computer processed checks sealed in budget envelopes.

So, although the forms of sacrifices and offerings vary dramatically between Old and New Testament worship, the need for them and the meaning they hold do not. Their foundation in Christ was once hidden; it is now plain. The Old Testament people offered their sacrifices to God on the more than eighty days a year that they consecrated to his worship. They gathered—not only on the Sabbath but also on festival days—to celebrate his goodness in creation and in salvation. The pilgrim festivals (Passover, Weeks, Tabernacles) were processions of singing, enthused worshipers. The weekly sabbath captured a holy harmony which later prophets associated with the Day of the Lord. Contrary to popular misperceptions, Old Testament worship was upbeat and joyful, at least that is how God intended it to be. The list of festivals reflects that joy.

Old Testament Festivals

Perhaps no facet of Old Testament worship captures its spiritual beauty and devotion to God as well as the Psalms. These songs, most of which were written by David, had been sung for centuries before someone—probably Ezra—gathered them into five hymnals for national worship. Some psalms express the pain and frustration of life in a sinful world, then end on a note of salvation and hope. Others are completely festive and celebrative. Because they fill the spectrum of the worshiper's moods, these songs are unsurpassed for use in worship even today. No other literature, spoken or sung, is as rich in religious nuances, as emotionally powerful, or as liturgically durable as the Psalms. The church that ignores them in its singing deprives itself of the best source of effective worship available to us.

THE SYNAGOGUE

As captives in Babylon the one thing the Jews missed more than any other was the temple—the place where they worshiped God. To fill that gap, the captives devised an alternative to the building in Jerusalem and called it the synagogue. That institution—a place of worship, a school, and a social center for the Jewish community—has had a profound and lasting influence on the Christian church's worship.

A synagogue could be founded wherever ten or more Jewish families gathered to worship. The assembly hall of a synagogue contained enough seats for its members, a lectern or pulpit for the leader, a seven-stemmed candlestick, and an ark filled with sacred scrolls. Services were simple: the group sang, prayed, read the Scriptures, listened to their exposition and application, and received the benediction.

Because Peter, Paul, and other New Testament believers continued to worship in synagogues after they became followers of Jesus Christ, it was inevitable that the synagogue model became the teaching-preaching part of the Christian service. Although temple sacrifices were eclipsed by Jesus Christ's sacrifice, Christian worship has followed the synagogue format for almost two thousand years. In fact, the visitor in our opening example would probably be more comfortable with a modern synagogue service than he would be with some ritualized forms of Christian worship. Even today the synagogue service is simple and direct. It is based on prayer, song, reading, and exposition.

Feast/Festival	Reference	Origin	Time Held	Purpose
Sabbath	Ex. 20:11 Lev. 23:3	creation	weekly, 7th day	rest for humans; worship of Creator
New Moon	Num. 28:11–15	Moses, 1300 BC	1st day of lunar month	special sacrifices of devotion
Trumpets	Num. 29:1–6	Moses 1300 BC	1st day of 7th lunar month	rest; sacrifices of devotion
Sabbatical Year	Lev. 25:1–7	Moses, 1300 BC	every 7th year	rest for the fields and ground
Year of Jubilee	Lev. 25:8–17	Moses, 1300 BC	every 50th year	liberty, justice, restoration of property
Day of Atonement	Lev. 16	Moses, 1300 BC	10th day, 7th, mo.	confession of national sin; atonement
Passover and Unleavened Bread	Ex. 12, Lev. 23:5–8	Exodus, 1350 BC	14th day, 1st. mo. for a week	celebrate deliverance from Egypt
Weeks/First-Fruits/Pentecost	Lev. 23:9–21	Moses, 1300 BC	50 days after Passover	thanksgiving for harvest
Tabernacles	Lev. 23:33–43	Moses, 1300 BC	15th day, 7th mo. for a week	autumn fruit harvest in tents as reminder of the wilderness
Purim	Esther 9	475 BC	13th day, 12th mo.	commemorate deliverance from Haman

Although Christian services followed the same pattern as synagogue services, the realities the two celebrated were quite different. Christ's name, Christ's Spirit, and Christ's supper revolutionized New Testament worship. Far more important than any practices or patterns the New Testament might mention, these three realities gave Christian worship a profoundly deeper dimension.

The name of Christ became integral to every element of worship. What the church receives, it receives in the name of Jesus. What the church does, it does in the name of Jesus. The church disciples, baptizes, and heals in the name of Jesus. When Christians pray, they pray in the name of Jesus, the ascended Intercessor. In fact, so basic is the name of Jesus to the church that Paul defines Christian saints as "all those who in every place call on the name of our Lord Jesus Christ" (1 Cor. 1:2). And Jesus tells us, "Where two or three are gathered in my name, I am there in the midst of them." Christian worship is effective precisely when it is convened, directed, and offered in the name of him for whose sake God hears and receives us.

Those who worship in Christ's name are those who have received his Spirit. The Spirit equips Christ's people with his gifts to better serve the Lord and one another (1 Cor. 12-14; Gal. 5: 22-23). Is it only coincidence that in one case after another in the book of Acts the Spirit falls on Christ's followers when they are together, presumably in an early form of New Testament worship? Undoubtedly not. Worship is the obvious context for the Spirit's most effective work.

Those who worship in Christ's name and receive his Spirit have communion together in the Lord's Supper. Celebrating the meal is worship— worship in which fellow Christians recognize that Christ and his Spirit bring them peace and reconcile them to God and each other.

These three realities—Christ's name, Spirit, and supper— are the foundation and substance of Christian worship. Many Christian churches claim New Testament support for other practices in their liturgies. Some believe that the New Testament prescribes footwashing, "passing the peace," or greeting each other with a holy kiss. Others teach that if the Spirit is present, Christians will speak in tongues and heal the sick. Many groups incorporate the greetings and the benedictions of the New Testament letters into the beginnings and closings of their worship services.

But although these practices are mentioned in the New Testament, and although they may add variety to a worship service, they cannot be equated with the three realities discussed earlier.

The New Testament does not contain a blueprint for worship. It is not concerned with liturgical precision and technicalities. Instead, the New Testament focuses our attention on broad ideas. It explicitly commands us to baptize and to commemorate the Lord's death in the supper. It reflects the continuity of Christianity with temple and synagogue worship. But because Christians of that day— particularly Jewish Christians—worshiped God in the threefold mode of temple, synagogue, and church, it is totally unrealistic to expect the Bible to prescribe a detailed pattern of Christian worship that would be binding for the church of all ages.

The Bible does tell us that it was difficult for the

early Christians to leave the trappings of their Jewish faith behind. Nearly thirty-five or forty years after Christ's ascension, the author of Hebrews still finds it necessary to assure believers that the high priesthood, the tabernacle and temple, and the ritual sacrifices were no longer necessary. Why make these points if for four decades the followers of Christ had been unshakably convinced of them? To return to Jewish worship patterns under pressure of persecution was apparently a live option in some parts of the church.

THE EARLY CHURCH

In the middle of the second century, a church father named Justin Martyr wrote the first step-by-step description of Christian worship. His service included the kiss of peace, the congregational amen, a benevolence offering following communion, and mixing the wine and water at communion. About sixty-five years later Hippolytus's *The Apostolic Tradition* elaborated on Justin's outline by providing the actual words for many parts of the service. Interestingly, many of the exchanges currently finding their way into Christian worship were present in Hippolytus's liturgy. The following is a good example.

> *Minister:* The Lord be with you.
> *People:* And with your spirit.
> *Minister:* Lift up your hearts.
> *People:* We lift them to the Lord.
> *Minister:* Let us give thanks to the Lord.
> *People:* It is fitting and right to do so.

This exchange contains the *sursum corda* (lifting of the heart), which became a cornerstone of Christian worship. Also present in this liturgy were the Pauline institution of the sacrament, the *anamnesis* ("Do this in remembrance of me."), and the *epiclesis* (prayer for the Spirit's presence). These elements and other liturgical details in *The Apostolic Tradition* gave the church something the New Testament had not provided—specific order and content for Christian worship. Many feel that this first complete liturgy should have a shaping influence on all subsequent Christian services. Hippolytus provided a base. But over the next two hundred years other church leaders greatly embellished the Christian service. Many of these additions seem overdone from today's perspective. The baptismal ritual, for example, was crammed with ceremonial flourishes. Those to be baptized were robed in white baptismal garments during a long private ceremony. Salt, the biblical symbol for cleansing, was touched to their lips. After the sacrament, these newly baptized Christians were anointed with oil—a token of the Spirit's reception—and given a mixture of milk and honey to drink—a rite which affirmed their participation in the promised land of God's grace. Obviously, although each of these practices had touchstones in Scripture, their correlation with baptism was forced.

The growth of ceremonialism occurred in both the Eastern and the Western churches throughout the ancient period. It affected ordination into holy orders, marriage, confirmation, last rites—in short, all the liturgical practices of the church. While the taste for elaborate rituals seemed to plateau in the early Middle Ages, it spurted again just before the Reformation.

REFORMS IN WORSHIP

The Protestant reformers, particularly John Calvin and the Reformed and Anabaptist strands of Protestantism, reacted to these ceremonial excesses by instituting a radical simplicity and directness into their services. Many of the Roman Catholic service's frills were either modified or discarded. Compare, for example, the Roman Catholic mass with the Lord's Supper as it is celebrated in most Calvinist churches today.

In their eagerness to rid their services of superfluities, however, some of the early reformers pared away the good with the bad. For example, many of them were as suspicious of the mass (a renewed offering of Christ) as they were of saint worship. And few of them agreed on exactly what should be included in a worship service. Calvin believed that the early reformers had been too hasty in limiting the celebration of the Lord's Supper. He sensed correctly that the early church had distinguished itself from the Jewish synagogue by partaking of the Lord's meal. But he was unsuccessful in convincing the Genevan church to celebrate the supper weekly— probably because many were afraid the people would continue to regard the supper as a mass.

Perhaps the best way to see how various styles of Protestant worship evolved is to study the origins of one of them. Dutch refugees in London and Germany were influenced initially by a Polish nobleman, John á Lasco. His Zwinglian leanings led him to highlight the Word and to minimize the sacrament in the liturgy. But his pattern of worship was tempered by a second leader, Peter Datheen, who—in collecting worship materials for the Dutch Reformed churches—borrowed heavily from the worship patterns of Heidelberg. Heidelberg, in turn, showed Genevan, French Reformed, Zwinglian, and German Lutheran influences. Hence, the worship of the Dutch churches after 1566 was a combination of many strands.

Surprisingly, in spite of such a wide number of influences, the Dutch service was a very simple one. Beginning with a votum and salutation, it included the use of the Decalogue as a teacher of sin, a general prayer, Scripture reading and sermon, psalm singing, and the Aaronic benediction. The Genevan practice of celebrating communion quarterly dominated. While there were slight variations in the order of worship from place to place, Datheen's basic service prevailed in Dutch Reformed churches and denominations until liturgical reflection became widespread in the twentieth century.

Given the long, complex history just surveyed, the need for guidance in understanding worship and shaping liturgy is obvious. Four principles provide that guidance.

First, worship must be biblical. The Bible establishes the need for worship, implies the nature of worship, and suggests the importance of specific practices. While we may not use the Bible as a liturgical handbook, it does teach us the importance of prayer, song, and offering, and it does command us to celebrate the sacraments. We should use the Bible as the starting point and the interpreter of Christian worship. Second, worship is universal. Every church, every denomination belongs to the "one, holy, catholic church." And every worship service should reflect that unity. Where worship conforms to the tried, established practices of the worldwide church, it avoids fads and trivia.

Third, worship must be confessional. While a church's confessions do not specify a liturgy, they should shape one. A Reformed service, for example, could never regard communion as a re-sacrifice of Christ. It's confessions demand that it treat the the sacrament liturgically as a meal of fellowship and remembrance. Fourth, worship is congregational. It belongs to the people in the local church and should express their immediate concerns and reasons for praise. Prayers, songs, and Scripture selections will reflect the congregation's needs. Even the style of the service will be conditioned by the character of the people in the congregation. Worship must be compatible with the people who offer it.

These four principles—not the multitude of secondary matters in terms of which most people judge—are the criteria of Christian worship. In planning and evaluating all worship, we must make sure it is biblical, universal, confessional, and congregational.

A. Personal Questions/Comments on Chapter 2

B. REVIEW OF WORSHIP PRACTICES

Summarize the main impact of the following on our worship today:

Old Testament worship

synagogue worship

New Testament worship

worship in the early church

the Protestant reformers

the Dutch worship services

C. STUDY OF PSALM 65

Psalm 65 illustrates how the richly nuanced worship of the Old Testament prepared the way for contemporary Christian worship. The psalm also demonstrates how worship in the Scriptures is always a matter of inner attitude and spiritual response, not merely an external exercise. Worship is basic; liturgy is its servant.

With that in mind, read Psalm 65 and list the many moods and responses of the worshiper it describes; for instance, in verse 1, *praise* is the worshiper's basic response, but *vows* are also mentioned, indicating that worship should be a time of rededication and renewal of commitment.

Jot down other responses and moods of the worshiper described in Psalm 65.

PREPARATION FOR WORSHIP

AS HER FAMILY SLID INTO THE FRONT pew, Mary Abbott glared at her teenage son, John. In spite of her repeated calling, pleading, and threatening, he had somehow still managed to wear socks that didn't match and a shirt stained with orange juice and egg. At least, Mary thought, the younger children looked presentable. Considering the chaos that had reigned in the Abbott kitchen and bathroom that morning, it was a miracle they were dressed at all. As the congregation rose for the first hymn, Mary barely moved her lips. As usual, Sunday morning preparations had left her emotionally frazzled and physically drained.

To Mary Abbott and many others like her worship has merely become part of a hectic routine. Instead of anticipating being in God's house and meeting with his people, many Christians rush around frantically on Sunday morning and arrive in the church parking lot feeling angry, tense, tired, and not at all ready to worship.

Proper preparation for worship is essential. If we were invited to lunch with a celebrity, we would plan our words and pick our clothes far in advance. How much more seriously we should take our meeting with the Lord!

The psalmist says "Be still, and know that I

50 am God" (Ps. 46:10). He suggests that a long pause from our routine is the best course to put us in close touch with God. Stillness makes room for God to enter, filling our hearts with his presence. So we must be still, "waiting on the Lord," recognizing that it may take some time and patience before we really know that God is with us. Through that stillness we prepare as individuals, congregations, and families to worship the Lord.

Personal Preparation

Perhaps the best way to prepare personally for worshiping God on the Lord's Day is by being a consistent disciple during the week. The writer of Proverbs says, "In all your ways acknowledge him, and he will make straight your paths" (Prov. 3:6). What we offer to God in the sanctuary is what we have been in the streets. Despite Sunday appearances, we cannot fool him. We are the same people in the pew that we have been on the job and in the home. So preparation for worship is basically a continuous, personal responsibility.

As part of that responsibility we must seek forgiveness and reconciliation with God and others. If the notes in our lives are discordant and out of tune, we will not be ready for the music of love and harmony in church. It won't ring true. That is why Jesus gave such elaborate detail on how to pursue reconciliation with a brother (Matt. 18:15–22). It is why Paul warned the Corinthians against celebrating the Lord's Supper "in an unworthy manner" (1 Cor. 11). Worship is for the reconciled. To prepare ourselves for Sunday worship we must confess our sins to God and to each other. As we learn to live close to God, to forgive and seek forgiveness, we will grow and mature spiritually. That maturity will enhance worship.

Since it is sometimes difficult to measure spiritual growth, a Christian should set goals. For example, if a Christian realizes that she has grown lazy in her love and service toward others, she might devote two afternoons a week to a diaconal project. If a Christian is nagged by doubts about election, he could read three good books on the subject and search the Scriptures. When the Deist Benjamin Franklin saw his morality slipping, he listed thirteen desirable virtues and daily checked his progress in attaining them. Reformed Christians ought to be even more deliberate and resolute in the pursuit of godliness. When we are, our communion with God is enriched and our worship becomes intensely meaningful.

It is also important that we anticipate Sunday worship. Because our lives are so full of demands and activities, it is imperative that we devise ways to put ourselves in the frame of mind and heart for meeting God. These ways might seem at first to be trivial rituals, but they can have big effects. For some it might mean polishing all the family's shoes on Saturday afternoon, for others preparing food for a family celebration on Sunday. For many European farmers' wives it means raking smooth the gravel around their homes late on Saturday afternoon. In small, seemingly meaningless ways like these, people discipline themselves to prepare for worship. They change the pace of their lives in anticipation of the next morning. Where such activities are accompanied by meditating on a psalm of worship before going to bed, by listing reasons to thank God in church, or by praying for the presence of the Spirit at the service, anticipation is heightened.

All of these things become futile, however, unless we make church attendance our top priority. We ought to be more religious about being in church than about sticking to our diets, swimming our laps, or doing our sit-ups. If we want to keep in spiritual shape, we must faithfully do our spiritual exercises. That means we should go to church even when—perhaps especially when—we do not feel like it. For although for the true, prepared Christian, worship will be predominantly joyful, thankful celebration, it is also part of the "service" we owe to God in Jesus Christ.

FAMILY PREPARATION

As parents stand at the baptismal font, they make some important promises about how they will raise the infant in their arms. They promise, first of all, to teach that child about God. What does that mean? Moses described it this way:

> "You shall teach them [God's Words] diligently to your children, and shall talk of them when you sit in your house, and when you walk by the way, and when you lie down, and when you rise. And you shall bind them as a sign upon your hand, and they shall be as frontlets between your eyes. And you shall write them on the doorposts of your house and on your gates."
>
> —Deuteronomy 6:7–9

Religious instruction ought to pervade the Christian home so that children learn not only about God's Word but also about how to worship that God. Parents should help their small children understand the worship service and its parts. They should explain why it is important to attend church. If a young child is trained "in the way he should go," the pattern of faithful worship is likely to be set for life (Prov. 22:6).

Such training should not involve threats or legalistic, condescending demands. They will only produce resentment in most children. Perhaps the best and most loving way to teach a child to value corporate worship is to involve her in preparing for it and help her participate in it. Talk with her about how she should groom herself for church and about the causes for which we give offerings. Help her understand the significance of the seasons in the liturgical year and the meaning of the words in the liturgy. Then be prepared for what might occur in the worship service itself. Parents should not hurry to take youngsters to church before they can sit relatively still, nor hesitate too long to take them out when they cannot. Parents also should not expect too much. Children are restless and must be given small ways—holding the hymnal, for example—to participate.

Of course, the whole burden of teaching children to love worship does not rest on the parents. The church has a responsibility too. Councils and consistories ought to be considerate enough to reserve seating near a rear exit for families with young children. Ministers ought to season sermons with illustrations and ought to address the children directly. Worship committees should plan music, banners, and movement that give children a sense of participating in the service. These options are certainly preferable either to ignoring children or to shuffling them out of the service at a prearranged time as though they were misfits in the worshiping community. Children belong with God's people. The Spirit uses their spontaneity and joyfulness to minister to more staid believers. Where churches have not given adequate thought and preparation to the childrens' involvement in worship, parents ought to press the issue with ministers and consistories.

Parents also should attempt to carry the celebration of God's victory over sin from the church to the home. The laughter of children, the happy sound of group singing around the piano, and the joy of welcoming married children and grandchildren to our table are consistent with the tone of Christian worship. Healthy family experiences should reinforce the worship experience and should foster a mood in which to return to God's house.

Vigorous, informed conversations on implications of the sermon are good Sunday fare, too. Families that read, reflect, and discuss exemplify responsible Christianity. Working out our salvation in the give-and-take of the family forum should have precedence over working out the crossword puzzle in the Sunday paper. What better use of the Lord's Day than to stimulate one another to responsible thought and action on ecology, nuclear disarmament, leisure time, or family relationships? The kingdom preached and prayed for in church is the kingdom which must come in our lives. Grappling with kingdom concerns stimulates us to repeated worship.

And what better day to deepen our fellowship with family and friends? Christian parents, busy all week, can share projects and healthy recreation with their children on a Sunday afternoon. Or the family can open their doors to brothers and sisters in the Lord—either friends or strangers—and celebrate together as fellow believers. When Sunday is over, the family should already be preparing for worship the next Sunday. Worship challenges us to serve the Lord in serving others. We can respond to that challenge as families by collecting for a charity, providing transportation for an aged neighbor, or volunteering for a community work project. Jesus' compassion and saving help to his contemporaries manifested God's reign, which arrived in Christ. God's rule continues through deeds of love and mercy by God's modern disciples.

Congregational Preparation

In 1903, a Reformed professor wrote a paper about worship. In it he asserted that "active participation in the worship service ought to be limited as little as possible to the activity of one man." The notion that worship can occur only through one man, he pointed out, is not consistent with the Protestant doctrine of the priesthood of all believers. Church members ought to announce songs and direct singing, the writer argued. They ought to explain collections, read the Scriptures,

offer prayer, or read the liturgical forms. The writer acknowledged that it would take time and careful planning to insure that such a service ran smoothly. It would demand extra work on the council's part, too, since they would have to approve each week's liturgy. But, he insisted, permitting members of the congregation to participate actively in the worship service would make the extra work worthwhile.

The professors's ideas may sound innovative to most Reformed ears, and with good reason. The concept of congregational responsibility for liturgical leadership has been muted in our churches. In many congregations little planning goes into the liturgy: the minister selects a few songs, the

organist selects a few pieces, and that's that. In such churches, the order of worship is so invariable that it can be printed on the back of the bulletin and remain unchanged for a year or two.

Fortunately, many Reformed and Presbyterian congregations are breaking away from routine in liturgy. They are appointing worship committees, people from the church who have a deep interest in meaningful worship services and the expertise needed to plan them. Musicians, artists, writers, ministers, elders, and deacons are working together to plan integrated, creative services. Each of these individuals brings his or her own spiritual gifts to the committee. For example, the minister or theologian steers the committee away from a theologically eclectic approach to worship. The trained musician articulates for the committee why certain pieces are suitable for a Reformed congregation and why others are not.

A well-functioning worship committee prepares for a service weeks before it is scheduled. They begin with a designated text and sermon theme, picked by the minister. All other elements of the liturgy are integrated into that framework. Members of the committee choose music and readings and prepare litanies of confession or thanksgiving. In time they select hymns and perhaps prepare bulletin notes on their authors or on the season of the year. They ask members of the congregation to serve as readers in a given wor-

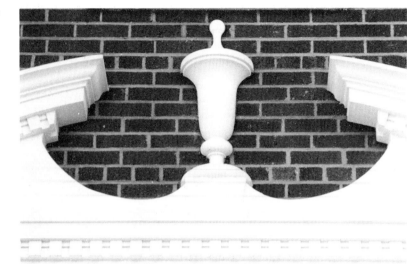

ship service, and they ask others to prepare banners for the sanctuary. (It is wise for a committee to remember that it is better to have a few, carefully crafted banners, changed just a few times a year, than many which exhibit sloppy thought and work.) It is also the responsibility of the committee to purchase bulletin covers, and often to plan and introduce offerings.

All of these elements need not be incorporated into every service. It would be too much. These are, rather, suggestions for giving variation and meaning to worship. Yet, as we shall see in the later chapters, the variation must occur within a constant framework of worship. And once a service is planned, it must not be subjected to last-minute changes—like having someone's Aunt Tillie who arrived in town Friday sing her favorite song at the morning service.

The resources for planning creative worship are increasing. Many denominations have appointed standing liturgical committees which produce worship materials and offer suggestions. Some have commissioned new hymnals and service books that contain helpful ideas. Liturgical conferences bring together musicians and others active on worship committees for workshops and presentations. *The Westminster Dictionary of Worship*, edited by J. G. Davies, also contains many excellent background essays on a wide range of topics. Frequent trips to Christian bookstores and perusal of catalogues from religious publishing houses will keep the alert worship committee fresh and supplied with more material than it can ever use.

Obviously the kind of planning just described places high demands on the time and commitment of members. It can reach a point of diminishing returns. And it can become a burden and a source of resentment if piled on the same, few people week after week. Worship committees function best where there are simple but explicit

organizational policies, a high level of commitment among members, and enough participants to spread assignments around. Turnover on these committees is desirable, thus enabling many members in the church to have a hands-on experience in planning a series of services.

Broad congregational planning for and participation in worship works effectively only where the entire congregation understands the reasons for it and wants it. Where this approach is new, it should only be undertaken for a clearly defined trial period. Then it should be honestly reviewed. Understandably, people with training, self-confidence, and experience in addressing others will feel more comfortable in active liturgical leadership. In communities with few such people, churches may be better served by a minister who takes a greater share of the responsibility for planning and conducting the services. Both positions are understandable and acceptable. In churches that have members of both inclinations some kind of compromise should be worked out. Liturgy should never become a source of division in a congregation. Those who are not inclined to take leadership should not resent those who are; those who are should not disparage those who are not. Here Paul's instructions about the different gifts which the Spirit grants different members is counsel worth pondering.

In summary, to play personal or family preparation off against congregational preparation would be a mistake. All three forms of preparation for worship which we have discussed are mutually complementary. None should be substituted for the others. When all three are vigorously pursued, the meeting of God with his people is certain to be a rich and inspiring experience for the church of Christ.

A. PERSONAL QUESTIONS/COMMENTS ON
CHAPTER 4

B. Bible Study

Read Deuteronomy 6:7–9

1. How have orthodox Jews interpreted these verses?

2. What, briefly, are these verses saying to Christian parents today, especially in view of the strong instructional role given to the institutional church?

3. Some of us can perhaps recall a vivid or unusual bit of religious instruction that we received from our parents. Think back to how your parents taught you to love the Lord and worship him. What impressions remain with you? Share some memories with the class. Can you draw any conclusions about how religious instruction seems to have been *best* given and learned?

C. Encouraging Each Other

Take a couple of minutes to list two or three impediments to worship on a personal or family level. If you've found ways to deal with these impediments, jot these solutions down too.

Then discuss what you've written with three or four others in your class. The purpose is to heighten awareness of common problems and to encourage each other to resolve those problems.

D. Worship Planning Committees

If you were a member of the worship planning committee in your church and the following proposals were presented, how would you react? Why? What key issue is involved in each proposal?

Proposal A—Young People's Service

The young people's society requests a Sunday evening "youth service" to be held on the Sunday following the denomination's annual youth convention. They ask that the pastor preach a sermon aimed at youth, and that members of the society read Scripture. Their society would also supply greeters, ushers, persons to take the offering, and special music. The president of the Society would offer the intercessory prayer, which would include petitions on youth-related needs and projects; and two volunteers would take five minutes each to present reports on special youth projects. A banner, which includes the words of Ecclesiastes 12:1a and the society's logo, would also be displayed.

Proposal B—Communion Service

One member of the worship committee proposes that the next communion service be celebrated in a different way. She suggests that after the sermon, prayer, and song, communicant members go to the fellowship hall, while the children and young people remain in the sanctuary for a special program on evangelism. Once in the fellowship hall, communicant members would sit at fourteen tables—one for each elder—and the minister would read from the form. Then each elder would break a loaf of bread in half, take a piece himself, and pass the halves down either side of the table. Each person could take as much as he or she wanted. Similarly, the elder at each table would pour out enough glasses of wine for everyone around his table. The breaking and pouring, eating and drinking, would all be done as the minister spoke appropriate words. After a prayer and a psalm of praise, the communicants would be dismissed.

The committee member also proposed that the bread be baked and the wine purchased by designated persons in the congregation. These elements could be presented at the beginning of the communion service.

Proposal C—The Sound of Music

One worship committee member strongly recommends that the services of Mabel Ivory, church organist, be terminated. Mabel has been playing the organ at nearly every morning service for the past twenty-three years. She owns nine arrangements of "The Old Rugged Cross" and plays each one twice a year for the offertory. The committee member points out that the congregation's tastes in music have changed since Mabel began as church organist; therefore she ought to be retired.

Proposal D—Liturgical Dance

Because people have been complaining that evening services are dull and too wordy, a committee member proposes that liturgical dance be a part of one evening service, just to see how the congregation likes the idea. After the greeting, a hymn, the creed, and an intercessory prayer, the minister would read Psalm 150. Then the local college's dance class and an eight-piece orchestra would give a "sermon-in-motion," interpreting the psalm. The service would conclude with a prayer, offering, hymn, and benediction.

THREE WORDS
OUT OF FOUR

CHAPTER FIVE

THUNDER AND LIGHTNING CIRCLED Mount Sinai as the people gathered at its base. Moses had told them God would speak from the mountain. He had warned them not to climb the mountain, not even to touch its borders. But he hadn't prepared them for the awesome presence of their God.

The people gazed uncertainly at the smoke-covered mountain before them. Was God on the mountain? Would they really hear his voice? Just then trumpets blasted through the camp. The ground shook. Children hid their faces in their mothers' robes. Grown men and women closed their eyes and trembled. "And God spoke all these words, saying . . . "

God spoke. His voice sounded through thunder and trumpets from the mountain. And the people were too frightened to listen. They pleaded with Moses to speak to God for them and to bring them God's Word.

God speaks to us today too. We may see no lightning and smoke and hear no thunder and trumpets, but God is speaking just the same. When we gather on Sunday, he greets us, pardons us, speaks to us through his Word, and gives us his benediction. Three of those four words—the greeting, pardon, and benediction—are the subject of this chapter.

The Greeting

Because God speaks to us in the worship service, it should be a time of reverence. From the moment the service begins, we should be attentive and respectful—listening to God's words and replying. When that moment is, however, has caused much debate over the years.

In some traditions a colorful procession of clergy clothed in elaborate vestments and carrying staffs and censors, followed by a choir singing an anthem, marked the beginning of the service. Some of our churches have liturgical processions today too: the minister, elders, and deacons enter together, or the choir enters singing. But the processional is not usually regarded as the beginning of a Reformed worship service.

Many organists and liturgists regard the prelude as the beginning of the service. And they have a point: in the spirit of the psalms, organ music can be conscious, direct praise to God. It can also be nothing more than mood music used to quiet the people down—and that hardly qualifies as worship proper.

Some say the service begins with the call to worship. Others claim that the call to worship, like a call to dinner, is not the real event. The reformers had some definite ideas about how a worship service should open. Luther began his services with a song. Others started with a prayer or an invocation: "In the name of the Father, the Son, and the Holy Spirit." Calvin and many who followed him believed that worship should begin with a votum and salutation. The votum, which some explain as the Latin word "dedication" (from *voveo*), states, "Our help is in the name of the Lord, who has made heaven and earth." It expresses the people's dependence on God.

The salutation is God's response—his greeting to the worshipers who are now ready to hear him.

The liturgical salutation is patterned after those found in New Testament letters. Paul's most common greeting to his readers was "Grace to you and peace from God the Father and the Lord Jesus Christ." While the Holy Spirit is not mentioned in the New Testament salutations, "in the fellowship of the Holy Spirit" is often added to the greeting at the beginning of worship to give it trinitarian completeness.

The greeting or salutation is more than a wish. It is a powerful word of God which brings about that which it states. It conveys the mercy, peace, and grace of God to the believing community. The minister of the Word raises his arm when he gives the greeting as a way of dramatizing and recognizing that the blessing-laden Word is falling on the assembled congregation. He keeps his eyes open—or, he should—because the greeting is not a prayer. We do not say hello to our friends by closing our eyes when we meet. Similarly, the greeting we exchange with God in worship should occur with wide-eyed expectation.

In some traditions the service did and does begin with the pastor and people greeting each other.

Minister: The Lord be with you.
People: And with your spirit.
　　or
Minister: Good morning
People: Good morning

This is followed by a salutation, invocation, or song of praise. In other words, the pastor and people greet each other before they together greet God and are greeted by him. The strength of Calvin's pattern —beginning with the greeting from God to his people—is that it avoids any sense of our being in church primarily to see or be with each other. It adds more solemnity to the service than an exchange between the worshipers themselves. But that does not mean the worshipers should not be involved in this part of the service. Responsively, the votum and salutation might read as follows:

> *Minister:* Our help is in the name of the Lord.
> *People:* Who made the heaven and the earth.
> *Minister:* Grace, mercy, and peace be to you from God the Father and from the Lord Jesus Christ, through the communion of the Holy Spirit (hand raised).
> *People:* Amen.

Begin with the greeting from God to his people— that's the primary thing. The divine greeting conveys God's grace, mercy, and peace to his assembled people. The congregational greeting is our response. This mutual greeting should never be omitted from Reformed worship services.

THE ASSURANCE OF PARDON

In that great classic of the Christian church, *The Confessions*, St. Augustine speaks about acknowledging our sins to God. His words are a penetrating rationale for including confession and assurance early in the worship service: "Who is the man who will reflect on his weakness, and yet dare to credit his chastity and innocence to his own powers, so that he loves you the less, as if he had little need for that mercy by which you forgive sins to those who turn to you?" (p. 74).

Those who confess their sin deepen their worship. They have more cause to adore God than those who neither admit guilt nor receive pardon. Honest, complete confession breaks down barriers, promoting communion and genuine worship. Therefore, an early expression of penitence enhances the tone of the entire service. Overwhelmed by grace, the forgiven sinner has an overriding desire to praise God.

Not all Christians agree that confession has a part in Christian worship, however. Some theologians have argued that because God's people are the reconciled community, they live in a state of grace. To dwell on sin, they insist, is to detract from Christ's victory and to rob worship of celebration.

This argument has historical weight. For the first thousand years of its history, the church did not include confession of sin in its liturgy. Confession was a private exercise that preceded the service. In the eleventh century the *confiteor*, a private, personal confession of sin made by the priest, was added to the beginning of the service. But worshipers still did their confessing privately, not in church.

What is wrong with excluding confession from worship? Such an exclusion ignores the need for daily conversion. Sanctification is a process. As long as the church is composed of Davids and Peters, of Corinthians and Galatians, it must teach its members when and how to confess their sins. As long as grace is dynamic, the church will be a reconciling as well as a reconciled community.

Many of the Protestant reformers saw it that way. They stressed the public, corporate character of confession and forgiveness and included them in the liturgy. This liturgical change reinforced ecclesiastical discipline. They discovered that the church where public confession of sin, acceptance of pardon, and rededication to Christ's service take place is also the church in which members encourage and exhort one another to a disciplined Christian life.

Perhaps the most Reformed way to structure a service of reconciliation is to begin by reading the summary of the Law. This approach, favored by Calvin, reflects the thought of the Heidelberg Catechism. The Catechism uses the summary to teach us "how great our sins and miseries are." By measuring us by our love for God and for others, the summary goes to the heart of our lives and compels us to deal with our motives and attitudes.

Many churches in the Reformed family prefer to begin the service of reconciliation by reading the Ten Commandments. This practice is consistent with the use of the Law as a teacher of sin, an understanding universally shared by Christians, but not particularly Reformed. Reformed theology views the Decalogue as a guide for grateful living. So while the Ten Commandments deserve a place in our liturgy, they are more appropriate after the assurance of pardon than they are as a call to confession. Calvin gave them this preferred position. And Abraham Kuyper, a nineteenth-century Dutch theologian, placed them even later in the service. He argued that the reading of the Decalogue was most appropriate after the sermon, just before the people left the church to live their obedience in the world.

The confession itself can take many forms: a printed prayer read in unison, a prayer offered by the minister or someone else, or an appropriate song. The Psalms are an especially good source of penitential songs for this part of worship. The confession of sins must avoid cliches or generalities, but must vividly and directly express the peoples' sins and sorrow for them.

Services that stop with confession of sin are liturgically incomplete. God's people must hear his gospel of forgiveness when they come to church. After they confess their sins, they must be unmistakably assured of pardon.

Perhaps the best assurance of pardon is a short Bible passage—spoken by the minister—a clear, uncompromising statement of God's grace, his forgiveness and acceptance of repentant sinners. Many churches instead have the congregation sing a song of assurance, but this practice is less than desirable. Singing is one of the major forms of congregational response in worship. But at this point in the service the people must hear directly from the Lord, not attempt to reassure each other. Even songs that speak clearly of divine forgiveness are less suitable than an appropriate passage read by the minister.

It is most effective liturgically to conclude the service of reconciliation with a declaration of pardon. Yet, often the dialogue between God and his church concludes with a statement of dedication. The Ten Commandments are very suitable for this purpose, especially when sung. So is another clear Old or New Testament formulation of God's will for his people's lives. Such a statement of dedication can be most effective if read by a member of the congregation.

An ideal Reformed service of confession and assurance, then, would be placed early in worship and would be close to what follows.

Summary of the Law (read by the minister)

Prayer of confession (by congregation, in unison)

Assurance of forgiveness (by minister)

Statement of dedication (Law, or appropriate substitute)

Of course, the content and the arrangement of the service of reconciliation should be varied to suit the liturgical season and the circumstances in the congregation.

An Amish mother, schooled only through the fifth or sixth grade, expressed the understanding and love that typify the spiritual purpose of this part of the liturgy. Noting that her three-year-old had grown unruly and disruptive, she neither threatened nor beat him. Rather, she quietly gathered him into her arms, held his face close to hers, and whispered words of correction and assurance into his ear. He went away quietly, eager to make his mother glad in him. So it is between God and the penitent believer.

THE BENEDICTION

The Christian worship service, particularly in its Reformed expression, concludes gloriously. It ends with a benediction.

The benediction has its roots in a covenantal act—the Old Testament blessing. When God, the covenantal head, gave his blessing to the patriarchs or to the people through Moses or the prophets, he was pledging that he would keep his promises. Thus, the Aaronic benediction, used in both Jewish and Christian services, is more than Aaron's wish or prayer. It is God's firm promise to give goodness, grace, and peace to his people.

> The Lord bless you and keep you;
> The Lord make his face to shine upon you,
> and be gracious to you;
> The Lord lift up his countenance upon you,
> and give you peace.
> —Numbers 6:24–26

The early church, influenced to some degree by the synagogue service, adopted the practice of concluding the service with a benediction. Sometimes they used the Aaronic blessing. At other times they used one of the benedictions from the New Testament letters. Among the fuller, more significant conclusions to the letters are the following.

The grace of the Lord Jesus Christ, and the love of God, and the fellowship of the Holy Spirit be with you all.
—2 Corinthians 13:14

Peace be to the brethren, and love with faith, from God the Father and the Lord Jesus Christ. Grace be with all who love our Lord Jesus Christ with love undying.
—Ephesians 6:23-24

Now may the God of peace who brought again from the dead our Lord Jesus, the great shepherd of the sheep, by the blood of the eternal covenant, equip you with everything good that you may do his will, working in you that which is pleasing in his sight, through Jesus Christ; to whom be glory for ever and ever. Amen.
—Hebrews 13:20-21

The blessing is not a sacrament. It does not work automatically or magically. Instead it is the pledged Word of the covenant God. When the worshiper has been a loving participant in the service, God sends him or her away with his Word of promise.

The blessing is in the same category liturgically as the greeting and the assurance of pardon—a creative Word that accomplishes what it states; a redemptive, reconciling Word that describes life renewed by God in Jesus Christ.

The power of a blessing is portrayed in the closing scenes of John Steinbeck's *East of Eden*. A young man sits at his father's bedside longing for forgiveness but not expecting it. Because of his jealousy and vengefulness, his brother is dead and his father paralyzed by a stoke. A household servant speaks with the father, urging him to bless his son, to lift his hand and move his lips as signs of forgiveness and acceptance. That is the only way, the servant pleads, that he can free his son from guilt's bondage and release him for creative and productive living.

We, too, need our Father's blessing. His benediction is the Word of hope and promise with which we reenter daily life, free of guilt and ready to live productive lives in his kingdom.

A. PERSONAL QUESTIONS/COMMENTS ON
CHAPTER 5

B. Our Congregation at Worship

1. *The Opening*

Examine your order of worship to determine precisely how your worship begins. Do the people and pastor exchange a greeting before God gives his word of greeting? At what point is there an exchange between God and his people? What words are typically used for the salutation?

What suggestions, if any, do you have for making this part of the service more meaningful or more worshipful?

2. *Confession/Assurance of Pardon*

Examine your order of worship to determine the content and sequence of the service of reconciliation. How does it compare to the four-part "ideal" Reformed service of confession and assurance described in chapter 5, just before the section on the benediction?

What form does the confession usually take? What Bible passages are commonly used for the assurance? What form does the dedication take?

What suggestions, if any, do you have for making this part of the service more meaningful or more worshipful?

3. *Benediction*

Recall what biblical benedictions your pastor used recently. Which of these speaks most powerfully to you personally. Why?

Is the benediction recognized as an important part of your service or is it viewed as merely a prelude to dismissal, a good time to slip on coats, hand Sunday school collection to kids, and so on?

What suggestions, if any, do you have for making this part of the service more meaningful or more worshipful?

C. Critique of Worship Situations

Read the following statements describing various worship situations and practices. Then, based on chapter 5 and your own judgment, decide whether each statement describes a "liturgically clear" or "liturgically muddled" situation. Be ready to defend your decisions.

1. *Bethel Church*

Bethel Church regular prays the following prayer of confession:

Dear Father, who loves truth and purity and who dwells in holiness, overcome the power of sin in our world. We experience the effects of the lie all around us. Life is full of filth and dirt. People no longer consecrate themselves to your service. But show us your mercy in Jesus Christ and deliver us for his sake. Amen.

2. *Peace Church*

The minister of Peace Church begins the morning service by rising and saying "Good morning." The people respond in kind. He then welcomes all the friends and visitors and invites the people to "pass the peace," which is explained in the bulletin. Next he announces the opening hymn. The congregation sings the hymn, then sits down for the prayer of invocation. The service of confession and assurance follows.

3. *Holy Trinity Church*

Holy Trinity concludes their service of confession and assurance with a responsive reading of the Ten Words or Decalogue. In this litany the leader (a lay person picked by the worship committee) reads each commandment as found in Exodus 20; the congregation responds with an affirmation of commitment taken directly from Scripture (Psalms or Prophets or Gospels or Epistles). For example:

Leader: "You shall have no other gods before me" (Ex. 20:3).

People: I will give thanks to the Lord with my whole heart, in the company of the upright, in the congregation (Ps. 111:1).

4. *Ebenezer Church*

Ebenezer takes its offering near the end of the service. It is followed by a song of dedication, the reading of an abbreviated form of the Decalogue, the *Gloria Patri*, and the benediction and postlude.

5. *Covenant Church*

The congregation at Covenant sings a hymn of praise at the end of worship. Then the minister offers this prayer:

Lord, we thank you for the blessings we have experienced here in your house. Now be with us in the homes, schools, factories, stores, and offices where we will serve you this week. Even there may we be favored by your presence. In Jesus' name, Amen.

The organist then begins the postlude and the people leave.

6. *Immanuel Church*

Following the summary of the Law and an appropriate psalm of confession, Immanuel's pastor says the following:

I now absolve all those who truly repent. I declare that all your sins are forgiven you, in the name of the Father, the Son, and the Holy Spirit. Amen.

READING AND PREACHING THE WORD

O F ALL THE POWERFUL, EIGH-teenth-century preachers, George Whitefield was among the most effective. Barred from pulpits in the Church of England, Whitefield proclaimed the gospel in fields and town squares. Often he spoke from the back of a horse, from a balcony, or from the grassy green of a hillside. So many people flocked to see him that he preached two or three times a day, every day of the week. He crisscrossed England, penetrated Scotland, and made three trips to America, bringing his message of personal renewal and complete trust in the sacrifice of Christ. Everywhere his message had the same effect: it produced softened hearts, wet eyes, and changed lives.

Another Calvinist preacher of that era, Jonathan Edwards, brought the same gospel with similar results— even though his delivery and methods were completely unlike Whitefield's. Instead of traveling from village to village, Edwards remained in his own pulpit. And while Whitefield's delivery was free and animated, Edwards was tied to his own notes and motionless as he spoke. Whitefield used vivid applications, Edwards brilliant logic. Yet both preachers brought a message that transformed the hearts of their listeners. The Calvinistic preaching of the two men contributed to a widespread spiritual awakening.

What this tale of two preachers reveals is that the power is in the Word, not in the style and gifts of ministers. God used Edwards and Whitefield—just as God uses the humblest country parson and the most publicized TV evangelist, the well-known theologian and the unnamed street preacher—for the same purpose: to bring his gospel. And then God's Spirit applies that Word, transforming the hearts of listeners.

Preaching and the Kingdom

Jesus was a preacher too. In fact, the first three Gospels all begin their descriptions of the public ministry of our Lord by mentioning his preaching (Matt. 4:17; Mark 1:14; Luke 4:14-30). Luke even tells the extended story of Jesus reading from Isaiah and preaching a sermon in Nazareth. For Jesus, preaching was an announcement of God's salvation. He was God's herald, sent to proclaim the arrival of God's kingdom.

Jesus' preaching was more than an explanation of God's work in someone else. It was a witness to what God was doing in and through himself. Jesus was God's Word of hope, love, and deliverance coming true. Thus, his preaching was a form of self-testimony. And his words and works were one. His words revealed the purpose and meaning of his saving works. His miracles and his death on the cross gave his words content and credibility. In part this is what lies behind the frequent expression "and he taught the people with authority, not as the scribes and Pharisees taught them." Jesus' preaching had power because it was backed up by his work. In him God's kingdom came. Through his continuing work, which includes the church's preaching, the kingdom will continue to come.

In the days after Jesus' resurrection and ascension, many brought the message of God's kingdom in Christ. The apostles were commissioned and sent with the message. New Testament prophets understood and applied the message to current issues. The evangelists brought good news to those who had not heard it before. The teachers explained it clearly and systematically. All told of Christ's works and teachings. They brought the gospel in the name of and therefore with the power of the One whom they pro-

claimed. By their gospel darkness was turned to light, aimlessness to purpose, despair to joy, fear to hope, sorrow to celebration, sin to service, and death to life. They preached the kingdom into reality.

Through preaching the kingdom comes into the hearts and lives of believers. God's rule and his glory become visible where Christians, gripped by the gospel of Christ, preach Christ grippingly. That is the message presented by a bronze plate attached to the pulpit in a suburban Chicago church. The plate is inscribed, "Sir, we would see Jesus." No preacher who reads and proclaims God's Word from that pulpit can escape the point: the only sermon worth hearing is one that announces with freshness and relevance the person and work of the Lord Jesus Christ.

DIMENSIONS OF PREACHING

Most people know when they hear good preaching. They know which sermons rouse their affections and which ones leave them cold as a stone in a winter field. Pastors have reputations as excellent preachers, as acceptable preachers, or as poor preachers. Word about them gets around quickly.

What is good preaching? Words used to describe it are "biblical," "powerful," "solidly Reformed," "fresh," "moving," "meaningful," or "relevant." It is difficult to give precise definitions to such terms, and rightly so. Because preaching is a tool of the Spirit, who blows where he chooses, and because it is also an art, it cannot be easily defined.

Some dimensions of preaching, however, can be isolated and discussed.

Preaching is announcement. It is an official recital of a new message. The New Testament's words for "preaching" and "preacher"—*heralding* and *herald*—make this clear. The herald (official) does not come with his own message, but with God's revealed (new) Word of grace in Christ (message). Thus, preaching which consists basically of the preacher's ideas and experiences, or even of the community's projects or the church's work, misses the mark. An effective herald of God announces what God says in his Word, the Bible, to his people in their present situation. He does not obscure or impede God's message.

Good preaching, then, must be biblically textual. It must be expository in the sense of exposing the text for the worshipers. It announces, "This is what God says to you today in the Bible."

Preaching produces inspiration. It blows life into dull hearts. It picks up lagging spirits. The "good news" of what God has done and is presently doing for his people inevitably has that effect. God did not send his Son to beat his people into the ground, but to lift them to heaven. The riches of the Christian's inheritance in Christ make the believer glad. And therefore preaching should be joyful, celebrating the goodness of God.

Preaching calls for conversion. Obviously, preaching must be honest to be credible. Honesty compels us to recognize that the kingdom is not complete and that salvation is a process. Preaching, then, exposes the evil forces that seduce us, tangle our relationships, and subvert society. It breaks through the barriers of our resistance to Christ's lordship. It probes beneath life's veneer and drives us to deal with what is there. Preaching exposes the effects of sin with such clarity that, in horror, we are led to hate evil and to repent. So whether it occurs in an evangelistic setting or in

74 an established congregation, preaching brings conversion. It effects a series of turn-arounds by which Christ pries us loose from Satan and joins us to himself. Real preaching never leaves people unchanged.

Preaching consists of instruction. Confessed in creeds, formulated in doctrines, explained in catechisms, the Christian faith is a profoundly teachable faith. It is faith based on the gospel—the great, new vision of the world and human life redeemed in Jesus Christ. Presenting it clearly and intelligibly has always been a high priority in preaching.

Organizationally, the Reformed tradition has singled out its teaching elders, theologians, and ministers of the Word as those through whom the community's faith is to be explained and defended. The Christian's most sustained, formative instruction in the gospel generally happens through the sermon. Consequently, clear-thinking, articulate Christians will welcome, as they always have, preaching that has a didactic or instructional dimension. Preachers should teach Christians from the Scriptures what God's plan of redemption is, how Christ has accomplished salvation, and what shape the new life should take in our age. Such teaching should be one purpose of every sermon.

Preaching has the dimension of ministry. Older language calls pastors "ministers of the Word." Ministers apply the gospel to the needs of their people. They do so in many ways and in various contexts: the counseling session, the classroom, family visits, graveyards, nursing homes, hospitals. But the most important place they minister to others is in the pulpit. Here they speak to all their people, every Sunday. To minister from the Word to a congregation, a preacher has to know his congregation. He must be aware of their struggles, understand their pains, experience their triumphs, listen to their complaints, share their ideals, and love them completely. He must be one

of them. Only then can he minister or apply God's Word to their lives.

Assessing the church in Ephesus and realizing how Timothy was struggling with it, Paul counseled the younger minister to be shaped by the Scriptures. He cited ways in which God's Word is profitable: "for teaching, for reproof, for correction, and for training in righteousness" (2 Tim. 3:16). These dimensions of Scripture's usefulness in Timothy's life correspond to the dimensions of the preached Word in the congregation's life. Where preaching is faithful and complete, it equips both individuals and congregations "for every good work."

Preaching is challenge. A sermon must call for commitment. It must arouse a desire to serve the Lord. It must provide direction in our lives. To be a disciple of Jesus means being a follower of the Lord. Our existence has movement towards a goal. The sermon appeals to hearers to press toward it.

Obviously one sermon will accent one dimension of good preaching more than another. Needs and circumstances will govern where the emphasis falls. But effective preaching will blend and balance all the dimensions to build up God's church in a given place. In time the richness and fullness of God's grace in Christ will be proclaimed.

Someone might wonder how people can worship by listening to a speaker. How does preaching the gospel ascribe worth to God?

As we suggested earlier, by listening to God speak through the sermon, we give him honor. He is the source of all wisdom and truth in Christ. As Creator and Redeemer, he has the right to speak. As his creatures and his children, we have the obligation to listen. In the sanctuary, then, God's role in our lives is made explicit. Hearing the Word gladly, but reverently, is a profound acknowledgment of who God is. As such it is worship.

Viewing preaching in that way lifts it far above the level of interpersonal dialogue. The sermon is not the insight or the opinion of a man whom we have hired and salaried to inspire, entertain, or enlighten us; it is God's Word. Through ministers God chooses to speak his Word with new grace and sharper bite. For this reason the church identifies, trains, and calls its ministers with care and deliberation. Where the church has lost the faith to see the minister as holding the divine office of God's spokesman, it robs itself of two things. It deprives itself of the likelihood of hearing God in the voice of the preacher. And it no longer sees the sermon as an act of worship.

In a more profound way the sermon as just explained is a stage in the drama of worship. It is a prelude to the sacrament, where grace is sealed and our relationship to God is confirmed. The sermon has the range and the flexibility to present the nuances of grace and to explain its implications. The sacraments seal that grace to us. Thus, sacraments are the culmination of the service. In a sense they are that for which preaching prepares us.

One student of Reformed worship notes that there are two kinds of preaching: evangelistic preaching and liturgical preaching. The two can be distinguished by the sacrament which each anticipates. Evangelistic preaching—reaching out

76 to the unconverted, unbelieving person—has baptism as its object. It concentrates on calling the church into existence. Liturgical preaching—edifying the established congregation—has the Lord's Supper as its object. It focuses on nurturing the people of God.

The explanation just given does not mean to suggest that there are two gospels or two kinds of grace. Nor does it deny that baptism strengthens the church's faith or that the Lord's Supper is a means by which divine grace enters our lives. Nor does it argue that there is no nurture in evangelism or no evangelizing in nurture. But it does show that the accents of the gospel fall differently in different contexts. Moreover, it illustrates that God's Word of grace is always sacramentally guaranteed.

If God is honored by our hearing the Word, he is also exalted by our participation in the sacraments which confirm it. Preaching and sacrament are not only bound to one another. They are both acts of worship.

THE READING OF GOD'S WORD

In a Reformed worship service the sermon does not stand by itself. It is bound to the Bible readings upon which it is based. Since the sermon explains, interprets, and applies the passages that are read, the Bible readings ought not to be separated from it in the liturgy. While reading and preaching the Word are two distinct activities in the worship service, they are integrally connected and complementary. The readings are the objective, enduring basis for the sermon. The preaching is the flexible, contemporary expounding of the Word. The one is the infallible standard by which the church measures itself. The other is the scrutinized, tested, yet authoritative attempt to present the Word in contemporary terms. But both serve the same liturgical purpose: helping God's people respond faithfully to him.

Lections Historically, the reading or readings of Scripture associated with the sermon or homily

have been known as the "lections." *Lection* comes from a Latin word meaning "reading." In more liturgically formal churches the *lectionary* is a book or collection of Bible readings for the liturgical cycle, or year. Churches that use a lectionary generally have at least two readings per Sunday—one from the Old Testament and one from the New Testament. In earlier periods of the church's history many congregations used an Old Testament reading, a reading from the epistles, a psalm response (sung), and a Gospel reading. This fuller pattern was not unknown in Reformed worship and is reappearing today.

Where lectionaries are employed, the readings for a given service are carefully selected for the

season or occasion in the church year. They are coordinated with the theme for that day. The readings are done by a "lector" who often is a lay person (although the priest or minister may give the Gospel reading). The Gospel reading is the last and most highly esteemed of the lections since it deals with the completion of redemption in the life and ministry of Christ.

Rituals replace preaching. The vocabulary we have been using indicates the significance which Bible reading has in Christian worship. That significance led earlier Christians to ritualize the readings in many churches. Ceremony eclipsed comprehension; doing replaced thinking; right practice superceded right teaching. In the Eastern Orthodox service, for example, the reading of the Gospel lection is still preceded by purifying the church with sacred incense. The priest and his assistants process around the congregation with the book held high for all to see, while clouds of smoke from the censer fill the sanctuary. The priest kisses the book as a sign of adoration of the Word. Yet, these services may skip from the ritualized reading directly to the eucharist or supper without explaining Scripture. For many centuries this ritual emphasis on the Word was adoration of a closed book. The Protestant reformers opened the book and discarded the ritual surrounding Bible readings. They dispensed with the gestures and movements in an attempt to accent the Word and the Word alone. The sermon was reborn as a means of grace in which the reading or readings were explained and applied. Since then a hymn, a short congregational response, or a prayer for illumination have been added to the Reformed reading of Scripture. But the emphasis falls on reading and preaching the Word.

Continuous reading Reformed churches have taken various approaches to reading the Scriptures. One preferred in the sixteenth century was the *lectio continua* or continuous reading of a book of the Bible. Each week the minister began where he had stopped reading the week before. His sermons were a series of messages following the progression within the book. Dr. Martyn Lloyd-Jones, a recent London minister with a reputation as an effective preacher, was noted for giving lengthy series of sermons on favorite portions of the Bible. His series on the Sermon on the Mount, on Romans, and on Ephesians were variations of the *lectio continua*.

The advantage of reading and preaching the Word according to this pattern is that it gives a systematic, coherent introduction to a part of God's Word. It also provides liturgical continuity from week to week. Obviously, however, it lacks seasonal flexibility. Today most Reformed and Presbyterian ministers prefer either to follow the Catechism and use the readings it dictates or to select weekly readings suitable for the liturgical seasons or for the themes and issues they wish to treat.

Who may read? Most Christians have misperceptions about who may publicly read the Bible in Reformed worship. Unexamined custom has produced the attitude that only ministers of the gospel may do so. This is a mistake. As in the synagogue and in many Christian churches, unordained people may read the Scriptures in worship. No liturgical or theological reason exists which prohibits men, women, young people, or even older, fluent children from reading the Word of God for the congregation. That worship belongs to the people of God argues for a variety of members as readers in worship. Their ability should be the basic standard by which they are selected.

Reading and preaching the Word are components in the covenant dialogue which structures worship—but they are only components. Talk about preaching as though it is the sum and substance of worship sells short the covenantal nature of our relationship with God. Because worship is a dialogue, a good sermon is enhanced by sensitive, appropriate responses structured into the liturgy. One of the best is a congregational amen at the end of the sermon.

On the other hand the importance of preaching must not be minimized. As one of the keys of the kingdom, preaching has the power to open and to close the kingdom of heaven. Through preaching and the work of the Holy Spirit, we come to know God. For "faith comes from hearing the message, and the message is heard through the Word of Christ" (Rom. 10:17).

A. PERSONAL QUESTIONS/COMMENTS ON
CHAPTER 6

B. DEFINING PREACHING

1. Having read about preaching in chapter 6 and, more significantly, having heard numerous sermons, what would you say is the *essence* of preaching? Try writing a definition in a sentence or two.

2. When the class has agreed on what the heart of preaching is, explore a few of the implications of your definition for preachers and for listeners.

C. EXAMINING A SERMON FROM ACTS

Read Paul's sermon and its context from Acts 13:13–52. To what extent are the six dimensions of preaching evident in Paul's sermon? Which dimensions dominate?

D. Examining a Contemporary Sermon

Talk about a recent sermon from your pastor, a sermon most of the class heard. Perhaps you can do this with your pastor present. Discuss how the six dimensions of preaching are evident in the sermon and which dimensions dominate. Perhaps the group also has some suggestions for more effective preaching and listening.

E. For Additional Discussion

1. Should young children leave during the sermon for their own children's church or should they remain with their parents throughout the entire service? Please give reasons for your answer.

2. Should the liturgy include a children's sermon? If so, what makes for an effective children's sermon?

3. Should preaching ever be eliminated from the evening service, perhaps replaced by a special program or a good film or some other activity? Why or why not?

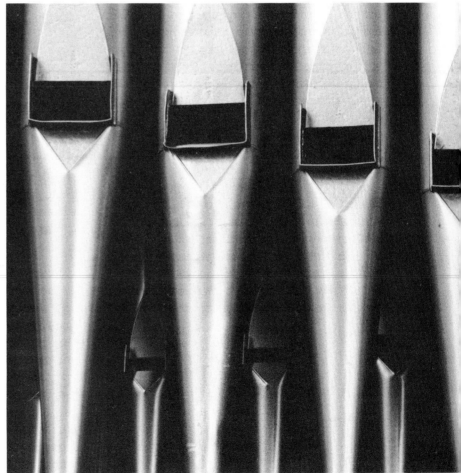

PRAYER AND SONG IN WORSHIP

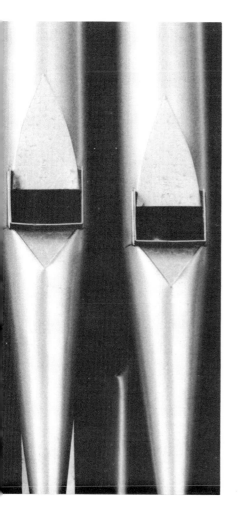

O N SUNDAY, APRIL 8, 1945, DIETRICH Bonhoeffer was executed by the German Gestapo. Hours before he died, he led a worship service for fellow prisoners; together they sang Luther's "A Mighty Fortress Is Our God." Minutes before his death, he knelt in fervent prayer. Then he was stripped, removed from the prison hut, and shot.

Later, a prisoner who had sung with Bonhoeffer testified to the incomparable spirituality of that final service. And the doctor who witnessed this condemned prisoner's prayer confessed that he had been unnerved by his devotion and his certainty of God's presence. Dietrich Bonhoeffer died with complete composure and serenity.

How is that possible? Through union with God in Christ. Bonhoeffer's song and prayer kept him there! United to God, he received Christ's salvation. It made him a conqueror.

As Bonhoeffer knew, prayer, both sung and unsung, is not an empty ritual or a mechanical response. It is a disciplined exercise in the life of one who cannot live outside God's presence. It is the spiritual activity by which God's children embrace him and through which they receive their benefits in Christ.

So it is really not surprising that Paul identifies

84 Christians as people who pray. He addresses the Corinthians as those "called to be saints together with all those who in every place call on the name of our Lord Jesus Christ, both their Lord and ours" (1 Cor. 1:2).

It's also not surprising that Christians *are* people who pray. Our lives have been renewed. Our existence has been transformed. And, as both Calvin and the Heidelberg Catechism teach, prayer is "the chief part of our gratitude." Prayer, whether spoken or sung, is an expression of thanks because it reflects the direction in which we are moving. Living in faithfulness, obedience, and service is the most profound way possible of saying thank you to God.

The Contours of Communion

Just as God's Word comes to us in many ways in the liturgy—in greeting or welcome, in forgiveness and assurance, in instruction and in benediction—so our response to him takes on different moods and tones.

The first tone is praise or adoration. This might be called "pure worship," for it ascribes worth to God as he is. It is directed toward his person. In the words of Augustine, "To know God is to love him." To praise God and to adore him acknowledge his incomparable greatness and sovereignty. Such worship is ecstasy in the true, legitimate sense of that word. For in praising and adoring God we "stand outside" ourselves, divested of all self-centeredness, and give him complete homage.

Thanksgiving is the second shape our response in worship takes. Here we turn from who God is to what God does. We thank him for all his blessings, acknowledging him as the source of all the goodness that we know, fully accepting our obligation to him.

The third mood is one of request or petition. Jesus taught us to address God as "Our Father." To be dependent on God is an inevitability of belonging to his creation. To admit our dependence is a gift of grace, the response of a new heart. As our Father, God gladly provides us with what is necessary and good. Thus, it is not presumptuous to make requests of him, or even to prevail upon him in our need. It is worship, for it recognizes the position he holds in our lives.

The fourth way in which believers respond to God's Word in worship is by confessing their sins to him. Unrecognized and unconfessed sin destroys communion. Confessing our sin, expressing repentance, and asking for forgiveness are painful, but unavoidable, parts of our communion with God. And they lead to deeper communion. For, humbled in confessing, we are more grateful. Grateful, we desire his presence more fully.

As our fifth and final response in worship, we commit ourselves to the Lord. We pledge him devotion, obedience, fidelity, and service. We offer ourselves to the One who has offered his Son on the cross for us and for our salvation. True dedication is verbalized and specific. We tell God that we will stop smoking on Tuesday and that we will work six hours each week at the church clothing distribution center.

Traditionally, the five contours of our communication with God have been taught to Reformed seminarians and explained to catechism students as necessary parts of the long or pastoral prayer. Careful study will reveal that they are recurring themes in the Psalms. They are also essential parts of the hymnody in a healthy church. They permeate worship like the aromas of a cooking dinner filter through the whole house.

There is no definite way in which the five flavors of our response to God ought to be structured into the worship service. The Bible offers suggestions. Church history and traditional practices give guidance. But, as we have seen before, the Bible is not a worship manual and the church's practice has varied. Both spoken and sung prayers, however, seem always to have been present in personal and corporate worship. How they have been used is instructive.

Corporate singing appears as early as Exodus 15, where Moses and the people praised God for delivering them from Pharoah. Group singing is clearly associated with festivals, marriages, and funerals in the Old Testament. David organized the Levites into choirs and orchestral groups for religious and temple ceremonies. These choirs and groups presented many of the Psalms as part of the worship service on feast and fast days.

The New Testament is also filled with examples of corporate singing. At the last supper Jesus and his disciples probably sang the *Hallel*as, Psalms 113-118, prescribed for the Passover feast (Matt. 26:30). Later the early Christians, the church in its infancy, praised God together (Acts 2:47). Paul instructed the Ephesians, in what is most likely a liturgical reference, to address "one another in psalms and hymns and spiritual songs, singing and making melody to the Lord with all your heart" (Eph. 5:19; see also Col. 3:16). Many chapters of the New Testament contain hymns: Romans 11:33-35; 1 Timothy 1:17, 3:16; Hebrews 1:3; Luke 2:4; Revelation 4:8; and dozens more. But the clearest suggestion of how singing occurred in a service is found in 1 Corinthians 14:26: "When you come together, each one has a hymn, a lesson, a revelation, a tongue, or an interpretation." Meager and incomplete as a liturgy, this text hints that Christian worship, like a syn-

agogue service, may have begun with group singing and the reading and teaching of God's Word.

The Bible also tells us a lot about spoken prayer. Many individuals, particularly prophets, "called on the name of the Lord." The frequent mention of prayers and sacrifices suggests that Old Testament priests were liturgical mediators who often prayed for the people while sacrificing.

Jesus taught his disciples to pray together. And the church of Acts did—often! Paul began most of his letters with a prayer of thanksgiving and exhorted his churches to pray. For example, 1 Timothy 2 is an extended, explicit chapter on congregational prayer in a worship service. But nowhere does the Bible tell us what kinds of prayers should be included in the liturgy or where they should be placed.

THE CHURCH'S PRACTICE

Only when we come to the early church or patristic period do we see how prayer is structured into the liturgy. We learn that the people stood during prayers of intercession and praise, and that a prayer reciting Christ's victory and asking for the Spirit's presence was offered with the Lord's Supper.

Singing is more difficult to isolate in the early liturgies, probably because, as a recent expert suggests, the line between speaking and singing or chanting was less distinct then than it is now. But early songs of glory and hallelujah do appear in the liturgy in connection with communion.

By the fourth and fifth centuries Christian praying and singing were becoming incredibly rich and complete. This development continued throughout the Middle Ages. The divine offices or hours, eight or more stipulated times for daily services of song and prayer, appeared. Special training emerged for cantors and choirs. In short, the trend in Christian worship from the fourth to the fifteenth centuries was from simplicity to complexity, from the congregation's involvement to the clergy's dominance, from participation to observation.

In the sixteenth century, Reformed worship returned to its patristic (pre-fourth century) roots, in order to reform its liturgy. One aspect of that reformation was a return to congregational song as the most appropriate form of music for worship. Another was a return to Scripture as the sole rule for faith and practice.

Consequently the Psalms, which had been prominent in all eras of Christian worship, took a central place in Reformed worship. The Psalms have been used as songs of praise, prayers of confession, responses to reading the Word, introits and calls to worship, and reinforcement in

pastoral prayers or sermons. They contain something for every liturgical situation. They powerfully and beautifully capture every religious mood. No wonder they have been indispensable in the church's worship.

John Calvin quickly saw how strategic the Psalms were for the purification of worship. He hired the best composers of his day and lured recognized poets from more lucrative positions to work on Geneva's Psalter. When the poet Marot died and Calvin needed a replacement, he convinced his coworker Theodore Beza to complete the versifications. With other reformers Calvin regarded sung psalms as prayers. Singing was an

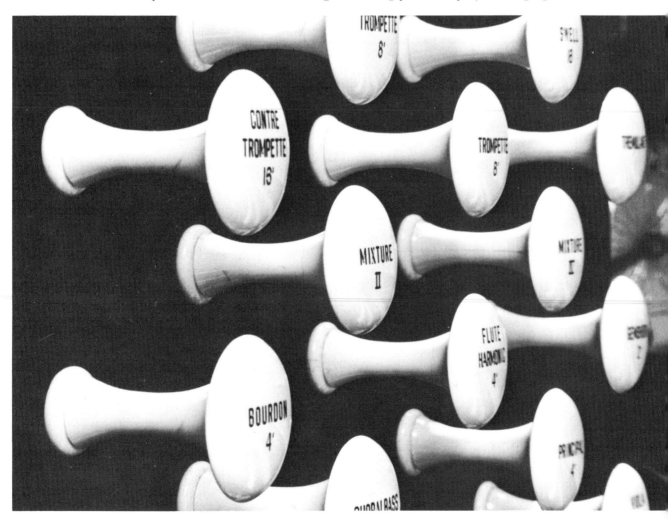

excellent way of addressing God, for it enlisted the emotions, united the people, and lifted worship to heaven with one voice.

THE REFORMATION AND LITURGY

If we were to attend a Reformed worship service in Switzerland, Germany, or the Netherlands in the late sixteenth or early seventeenth century, we would experience prayer and song as follows. Early in the service a song leader (*voorzanger*) would announce a psalm of praise. He would sing the words and melody line by line; we would repeat each line after him. And we would do so in unison, without the organ. (Both singing in parts and with accompaniment were banned.) We would use a recent translation and a musical rendition familiar and up-to-date. Later in the service we would kneel or perhaps stand for a long pastoral prayer which the minister would read. The prayer would always be virtually the same unless the minister was preaching a catechism sermon. The service would close with a psalm of thanks, again led by a song leader.

Worship, then, that had been "re-formed" was drastically different from what had come before. It also excluded many of the things that are familiar parts of our liturgy today—such things as our preludes, postludes, offertories, hymns, hymnsings, prayer concerns, ministerial freedom in prayer, and a variety of other items.

SONG AND PRAYER TODAY

Today Reformed and Presbyterian singing and praying show the marks of 450 years of change.

Organs were introduced before 1650. Kneeling, which was never tolerated among English Puritans or Scottish Presbyterians, disappeared in the Netherlands about the time women began carrying stoves of hot coals to church and using them to prop their feet off the cold, slate floors. Hymns crept into services when German, English, and American proponents of piety and revival wrote them by the thousands. Few denominations now exclude them. Extemporaneous prayer and testimonies were admitted for the same reason that hymns were.

The trend now is to employ many shorter, focused prayers rather than the proverbial "long prayer." Interestingly, prayers are once again being written out beforehand and read in the service.

Choirs are largely an American, twentieth-century development in Reformed worship. Just as one person, usually the minister, voices a prayer on behalf of the congregation, so too the choir or other muscisians may sing on behalf of the whole congregation. Recent developments reveal a growing variety of solo and group singers and instrumentalists in worship.

Nonetheless, the history of the church makes a warning in order. Most of the actions of the people should most of the time be said or sung by the people themselves, not by the minister or the choir. Otherwise, the members of the congregation no longer see that these are *their* actions whereby *they* express *their* faith. They begin to think of them as actions of the choir, or of the minister, and they begin to think of themselves as spectators at a performance. With fierce jealousy the people must guard their response in worship.

Warnings such as this one are often necessary in a time of change and experimentation in the liturgy. Whether the changes have been from "thee" to "you" in prayer, or from organs to guitars in music, they have usually occasioned discussion, disagreement, and frustration. But worship that belongs to the people must always be in their idiom. The contours of our communion with God are adaptable to a wide range of cultural forms. What is essential is that the forms serve the five features of worship and not inhibit them.

Is Singing Praying?

At first glance it may appear that those who argue that all song is prayer are correct. Many of our psalms and hymns address God or Christ directly.

> Do not forsake me, O my God.
> Do not go far from me, O Lord.
> Come quickly, help me now, I pray,
> O Lord, my Savior and my God.
> —from Psalm 38

"Have Thine Own Way, Lord," "I Need Thee Every Hour," and "O Sacred Head, Now Wounded" are other examples of such hymns.

Many hymns and psalms, however, are not addressed directly to God. Some of them are meditative or reflective. Through singing them, the participant cultivates his devoutness or her inner reflection on God. For example:

> How blest are those who fear the Lord,
> and greatly love God's holy will;
> Their children share the great reward,
> and blessings all their days shall fill.
> —from Psalm 112

Many hymns fall into this category. Liturgically they have the potential of being used as confession, testimony, or even a form of proclamation.

> God moves in a mysterious way,
> his wonders to perform.
> He plants his footsteps in the sea,
> and rides upon the storm.

Still other psalms and songs are an exercise in mutual exhortation. Psalm 47, which is the basis of "Praise the Lord Ye Lands," and "Exalt the Lord, His Praise Proclaim" from Psalm 135 are examples. Hymns of this variety are "Stand Up, Stand Up for Jesus," "Rejoice, Ye Pure in Heart," and "God Be with You Till We Meet Again." By stretching the definition of prayer, one might argue that communion with God as well as with one another occurs in these numbers. But such psalms and hymns are not prayer in the strict or usual sense.

The sensitive worshiper and the careful liturgist will take account of these differences in psalms and hymns.

Kinds of Prayer in Worship

Some prayers that might appear in a modern Reformed worship service are worth noting, defining, and commenting on.

The *invocation* is a brief opening prayer which invites or invokes God's presence and blessing. Standard fare in Presbyterian services, it is often replaced with God's greeting, a silent prayer, or both in Reformed churches. The Reformed rationalization is that God does not have to be invited to a meeting that is convened at his command.

A *prayer of confession* acknowledges the people's sin, asks for pardon on the basis of Christ's sacrifice, and solicits reconciliation. It is sung, prayed in unison, or spoken by someone, usually the pastor.

The *pastoral* or *congregational prayer* voices the concerns and needs of the church. It focuses on the ministry and programs of the congregation, denomination, and world church. It also intercedes for members in special circumstances and includes petitions for all people and world affairs. It is usually an abbreviation of the long or general prayer, which in the past also included statements of praise, thanks, and confession.

A *prayer for illumination* precedes the reading and preaching of the Word. It asks for the Spirit's work—clear heads, open hearts, and effective proclamation.

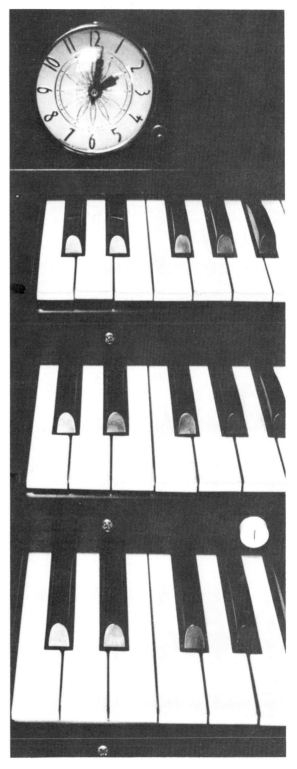

A *litany* is a highly stylized, antiphonal prayer in which both the leader and congregation address God in turn. The petitions of each party are correlated. This form of prayer is usually reserved for special services or the Lord's Supper. Responsive readings of the Law or the Catechism are not litanies.

Sometimes one hears about *collects*. *Collect* refers to a style of prayer rather than to the occasion for prayer in the service. The term refers to the collected prayers of all present. Traditionally, there was a brief pause between the invitation to pray and the prayer itself so that people could "collect" their thoughts. The collect consists of an address to God, a clause recognizing one of his accomplishments or attributes, and a brief petition. It can be used in invocation, confession, application, or for illumination.

GOD'S PEOPLE RESPOND

Prayers and songs, then, are the two basic, constant ways that the people respond in worship. Reformed worship makes clear that these are the congregation's responses to God's Word. They are not the private activities of pastors or performers. By singing and praying, God's people become fully involved in the worship dialogue. Both praying and singing are adaptable to each subsequent stage in the progressing drama of the service. Their biblical richness, historical variety, and liturgical flexibility give Reformed worship the ability to express the participant's response with depth and feeling. Because both forms are direct and plain, they enable worshipers to be full participants.

A. Personal Questions/Comments on
Chapter 7

1. Using a bulletin and your church's hymnal, look back at the songs used during a recent worship service. Read through the songs, then classify each according to the three categories described in chapter 7:

   —songs that address God directly (prayers)
   —songs that are meditative, reflective
   —songs that mutually exhort

   Are the types of songs appropriately incorporated into the worship service? Which type dominates? Which type is used least or not at all? What posture is appropriate to each type?

2. The following are excerpts from articles by members of the Psalter Hymnal Revision Committee. To what extent do you agree with the statements?

   "A good hymn should not be primarily a vehicle for individuals but should be a vehicle for the worship of the entire believing community. A hymn may indeed express the feelings or describe the experiences of an individual, but it should not do so in such a way that the congregation cannot join the individual in worship. An outstanding example of an individualistic hymn is 'In the Garden,' 'And the joy we [Christ and I] share as we tarry there, None other has ever known.' "

   —Anthony A. Hoekema

   ". . . Fanny Crosby's sentimental hymns are old favorites with many people, and their texts are fairly biblical—although Reformed believers don't usually like to talk about 'raptured souls resting beyond the river.' 'Jesus, Lover of My Soul, Let Me to Thy Bosom Fly,' is also an old favorite. But that hymn sounds like this to a stranger or a teenager in the 1980s: 'Forsooth, sirrah! the countenance of yonder lordship, Jesu hight, doth commend itself for counsel sweet.' Such language, Klaas Schilder would say, is closer to the language in which the Roman Catholic Church used to worship than to the direct, gritty speech of the open Bible translated by Luther. Can we afford to be out-of-date in our songs . . . ?"

   —Calvin Seerveld

   "Music should rank last in a listing of the aspects of our hymns. The message of the hymn should rank first. Close behind should come the theology of that message . . . . Next comes the effectiveness of the words used to convey the theological message . . . . Following all these, as supporting servant, should be music. Although many of us profess that music ranks low, in our actual practice of hymn singing, I fear that we too often elevate music to the highest position."

   —Dale Topp

"What about items in the denominational hymnbook that offend one or another sector of the church? . . . Many Northern American Christians from a variety of European backgrounds can sing with sincerity:

We praise Thee, O God, for thy guiding hand,

In leading Thy Church to freedom's fair land;

Through sore persecution our fathers here came,

Where free and unfettered, they worshiped Thy name.

It is patently not true for Black North Americans that their ancestors came 'free and unfettered' or that this continent was for them 'freedom's fair land.' Of course we would never sing this song in the Garfield CRC. But is this enough . . . ? In this case, I contend, the denominational hymnal would not suffer from a deletion of this stanza."   —Jack Reiffer

1. If prayer is a response of the congregation, what part should the people have in offering a congregational prayer? When and how should prayer requests be made? Who should offer the prayer? Should a written prayer, form prayer, or an extemporaneous prayer be used?

2. Should silent prayer, essentially an individual act, be part of corporate worship? Why or why not?

WORSHIP AS COMMITMENT

CHAPTER EIGHT

W HEN MOTHER TERESA TELLS PEO-
ple she is a Christian, they understand clearly that Christian commitment is an extremely serious
matter. Mother Teresa ministers to India's dying
and destitute, to the tiny baby abandoned on a
garbage heap, to bodies rotting with cancerous
sores—to the people no one else will touch. "For
me," says Mother Teresa, "each one is an individual. I can give my whole heart to that person for
that moment in an exchange of love. It is not
social work. We must love each other. It demands
emotional involvement."

Few of us are as faithful in our commitment to
God and others as is Mother Teresa. We need to
be prodded and reminded from time to time. Our
commitment needs renewing and reinforcing.
One of the ways we receive that renewal is through
worship. In the worship service God reaffirms his
love and commitment to us through his Word,
and we respond. We commit ourselves to God
again through the creed, the law, the offering,
and sometimes through vows.

THE CREED: TOTAL DEDICATION

The creed moves around liturgically. It is the
liturgical gypsy. Sometimes it appears in morning
worship, sometimes in the evening service. Some-

times it takes the form of the Apostles' Creed, sometimes the Nicene Creed, and sometimes the Athanasian Creed. The creed has been read by the minister, sung by the people, or recited in unison. It has been spoken after the assurance of pardon, recited just before the benediction, or confessed at the Lord's Supper.

Despite the above variety and movement, the creed always serves the same liturgical function. It expresses the people's total dedication to God. At first thought this seems strange. The creed is a summary of the Word. It recites the core of God's redemptive revelation in Scripture. Consequently, it might be more appropriate to regard it as something God says rather than something the people speak.

But while it is true that the creed is a summary of the Bible, it is still primarily a confession. By confessing it, the people state that they appropriate the Word. They admit that the Word is gospel for their lives. They affirm that the whole Word of God is the only Word by which they can and will live. So when the church speaks the creed, it explains its faith. It gives its corporate testimony.

Unfortunately the church often says the creed ritualistically or in monotone. There is no zing in the people's voices; there is no light in their eyes. If they understood what they were saying and believed in what they were doing, maybe this would not be so. They should be making a ringing affirmation of their faith, not reciting cold facts.

Perhaps if Christians considered the circumstances under which others have confessed their faith, they would profess the creed with greater conviction. In 1981, for example, Roman Catholic Archbishop Romaro was gunned down at his altar for boldy confessing his faith on behalf of El Salvador's poor. Hundreds of years earlier Protestants had their tongues ripped out to prevent them from testifying to their faith as they were being executed.

Considering these stories and thousands of others like them should help Christians see how remarkable it is that the creed is now a vital part of every worship service—and also how remarkable the creed itself is. That it is said by God's people in unison makes the creed more eloquent than the testimony of any individual Christian, however inspiring his statement may be. That it is so comprehensive makes it more profound. That it is confessed corporately makes it more powerful.

Thus, while it took five centuries for the creed to find its way into Christian worship, it should never be removed. Where it is placed is less crucial, although a location near the end of the service seems most appropriate. Which creed is used is also secondary, although the Apostles' Creed— the most memorable and least polemical of the three—should receive pride of place.

The Offering: Selfless Commitment

At its best, the Christian community has been selfless. It has served others with its time, energies, and resources no matter what the cost to itself. In the early church Christians were known for their kindness to slaves and prisoners. Unlike their fleeing neighbors, they often stayed behind in plague-infested cities to bathe fevered foreheads, feed the weak, and bury the dead. Monks and nuns bound themselves with vows in order to free their lives for Christian charity.

Today Christians continue to give of themselves. Some serve as short-term volunteers or promote development in new nations. Others, like Mother Teresa, devote their whole lives to helping the needy. Still others support such ministries through the offering each week. If the creed is a liturgical way of saying "We will love the Lord our God with all our heart, and mind, and strength," the offering is a rite which affirms "and our neighbor as ourself!" It is important that we respond to God's Word by telling him that we are selflessly committed to others, for Christ's sake.

However, it is not only or even first of all the poverty and suffering of other human beings that motivates Christian selflessness. Compassion in Christ is part of the new order. It is stirred up in hearts renewed by the Spirit. And it is even provided with God's where-with-all. Paul says," And God is able to provide you with every blessing in abundance, so that you may always have enough of everything and may provide in abundance for every good work" (2 Cor. 9:8). Thus, both the motive and the resources for giving to others are the work of God. That is why the expression of Christian selflessness begins in the sanctuary and not in the streets. Christians give what they have received. They also give because they have received.

Ourselves or others? For which causes may the church legitimately collect money? Benevolence towards those in our own community or on the other side of the world obviously qualifies. But some argue that support for local programs, buildings, and salaries does not. Such support is not, they argue, selfless giving, but rather self-preservation.

Others point out convincingly that collecting money for the local congregation's program bears a dimension of selflessness. Preaching repentance and the new life has tremendous social effects. It fosters responsible workers, creates generous employers, produces safer streets, and builds a sense of community. To support preaching from our own pulpit, therefore, is a contribution to all those around us. Similarly, the educational program instills values, vision, and faith in the next generation; this is a contribution to those who

98 come after us. The resources of the church, its building, its ministry, and its prayers also benefit nonmembers.

A good general guideline might be that half the local church's budget should be for the congregation's own programs, and half for regional, national, and global programs. Building programs should be additional.

How much? The offering is a ritual pledge that all we have is dedicated to God's service. That does not mean we should put everything entrusted to us into the collection plate. But just how much we should contribute is something Christians often do not agree on.

Many congregations are finding it archaic, even offensive, to use a per-family-per-week quota. This approach may have worked when there was relative economic parity within the church. But that is usually not the case today. Instead, many churches are now asking members to contribute a percentage of their adjusted gross income. What percentage should that be? Tithing is still an excellent general guideline, although some can and should give far more than 10 percent while others may not be able to reach that level. In any case, the local congregation should never control the full 10 percent of its member's income. Individuals and families must have the satisfaction and blessing of discretionary giving to causes important to them.

More than money Commitment of financial resources is only liturgically symbolic of self-commitment to the Lord and his programs. The offering should be accompanied by the presentation of other resources—such as time, abilities, and services—to local or denominational projects and should be structured into the service as an integral part of a broader service of dedication.

In the same light deacons should be more than collectors and counters of money. They should function as resource brokers in a congregation. They should compile data on congregational gifts, be vigilant toward needs, evaluate causes perceptively, allocate resources, and counsel the destitute. Deacons are called to show Christ's mercy to the church and the world.

The Law: Grateful Commitment

Liturgically the Ten Commandments belong to the service of dedication— near the end of worship, after the Word has been explained and applied. When it has been inspired and challenged, the church is ready to recommit itself to God's service.

Historically, however, the Law has come after the assurance of pardon or the absolution as a guide for the saved. Calvin incorporated it here. He had the people sing the Decalogue.

Today there is much resistance to reading the Ten Commandments in Reformed worship, but dispensing with them would be a great loss. The creed, the Lord's Prayer, and the Decalogue have been the three mainstays of Christian instruction and Reformed liturgy. They have shaped the church. All three should continue to do so. It is arbitrary to dismiss one as liturgical drudgery and a mere formality while retaining the other two!

Nonetheless, Reformed worship should use the Law with more vitality than it has in the past. The people should read or recite it as their statement of dedication. At the very least they should affirm it in a litany. Several useful ones exist. At appropriate seasons or in some thematic services another Bible passage can be substituted for the Ten Commandments. But the Decalogue's pres-

ence should remain dominant and pronounced in Reformed worship.

Significant times in believers' lives call for public vows—for affirming their responsibilities toward the Christian community. That this happens in a liturgical setting indicates that it is an act of commitment. Done in the presence of God's people, these acts of commitment enhance the well-being of the body of believers. The vow becomes part of the person's and of the church's response to God.

Vows are taken "before God and in the presence of these witnesses." They include public profession of faith, ordination and installation of officebearers, baptism vows, and in some cases, marriage vows.

Profession of faith Rampant confusion exists about the exact nature of public profession of faith. It is not an act of joining the church. Rather it is acceptance of the responsibilities of membership. The person making profession usually has been a member of God's people since birth. That membership was sealed in baptism. But now the young person vows to live as a faithful, responsible, constructive member of the church. Obligations do not begin with profession—no more than blessings do; they are simply recognized and accepted in that ceremony. And be-cause this pledge is significant for the con-gregation, it is sealed before them by solemn vows.

The full examination of the professing member used to occur in front of the whole congregation. It was a free and flexible ceremony. The professing member was asked a series of questions covering the person's faith commitment, knowledge of the gospel, and submission to the judgment or discipline of the church. Today, although professing members appear in front of the consistory instead of the whole congregation and although the ceremony itself is structured by form and liturgy, conditions of responsible membership remain the same.

Ordination Ordination vows obligate a person to special service in the church. The church calls people for specific functions or ministries which it regards as its responsibilities. These include minister of the Word, professor of theology, missionary, evangelist, elder, and deacon. A person being installed in one of these offices makes certain vows, parelleling closely the vows made for profession of faith. The first affirms that the person feels called by God and the church to the office; the second that the teachings of the Bible and the church are true; the third that he will be loyal to his charge and submissive to the church in conducting his duties.

The church carries on some of its most essential duties through people who commit themselves to these special offices.

Baptism Parents who present their child at the font commit themselves to building the church of tomorrow. This work is so strategic for God's ongoing program and for the salvation of children, that this commitment is also reinforced by liturgical vows. The parents vow that the child is a sinner needing grace and that the gospel of Christ is her only hope, and that they will raise the child to know and serve the Lord. While the sacrament of baptism entails much more than parental vows, it certainly includes them.

Marriage Technically a marriage is a legal transaction under the authority of the state. The state extends its authority to ministers of the gospel to join a man and a woman in matrimony. This concession is rooted in a sacramental understanding of marriage in the Christian West. For centuries the church was regarded as the institution which ministered God's grace to a couple joined in marriage.

While the Reformed tradition broke with the notion of marriage as a sacrament, it retained a deep sense of the church's stake in strong marriages. In the earliest Reformed rites, therefore, marriage forms or ceremonies were included. Often the church felt so deeply about the necessity of marrying in the Lord, that marriage vows were exchanged at the conclusion of a Sunday worship service. While marriage is seldom a part of worship services today, Reformed people still believe weddings should take place in church and that a minister should perform the ceremony. Once again, a deep sense of commitment to God permeates the taking of vows.

THE COMMUNITY OF THE COMMITTED

Human life is littered with broken commitments. Most of the pain and mistrust in our existence, both as nations and as persons, stem from them.

The church is the community of the committed. The ability to make and to hold commitments is a work of grace, belonging to God's kingdom in Christ. The church is committed only because God, their Father, is. His commitment is a redemptive one; the church's is a grateful one. The church's commitment, then, is God's shovel for clearing much rubble out of our lives.

The liturgy is, among other things, a weekly exercise in recommitment. As such it is essential to the rest of life—to marriages, to business deals, to taking tests, to basketball games, to child rearing, and to friendships. Erratic, undisciplined participation in Christian worship undermines our commitment to God. The erosion of the rest of life cannot be far behind. Commitment to God and commitment to others stand together. While church attendance is no guarantee of genuine commitment, either to God or to others, the liturgy is God's appointed means for expressing and renewing our commitment to him.

A. PERSONAL QUESTIONS/COMMENTS ON
CHAPTER 8

Try the following activity for an interesting way to apply the chapters on the four Words from God and the people's response in song, prayer, and commitment (chapters 5–8). For a more traditional approach (to chapter 8 only) see section C.

Imagine (again!) that you are a member of the worship committee and that it's your turn to draw up a complete liturgy for next Sunday's morning service. The pastor has told you he'll be preaching on Psalm 23 and John 10:11. As an experiment, he's asking the worship committee to decide the order and content of the remainder of the service. You may organize your liturgy around the following general headings or start from scratch, as you wish. The questions under each heading may help you decide what to include. The task is not to answer the questions but to draw up as specific a liturgy as time permits.

The Opening

Who will preside? What will that person say? What will the people say? What song, if any, will the congregation sing? If you can't name a song, perhaps you can suggest one of the three types of songs.

Confession and Assurance

What form will the confession and assurance take? Will the Law be read here or elsewhere? Who will read it or how will it be presented? How will the congregation respond to the assurance from God? What song, if any, will they sing?

Proclamation of the Word

Who will read the Scripture? What prayers will be included in this segment of the service? How will the children be addressed?

The Response

Will the offering be taken here? Who will give the offertory prayer? Could the Law be read here? The creed recited? What song, if any, will the congregation sing?

The Dismissal

What benediction will be used? Will the people respond in any way?

After the exercise, you may want to talk about possible changes you'd like to see introduced into the liturgy of your own congregation.

1. What are your reactions to the weekly reciting of the Apostles' Creed (or other creeds) in the worship service? At what point in the liturgy is the creed usually recited? Does the congregation generally seem to react positively or indifferently to the creed? Any suggestions for making the recitation of the creed more of a confession and less of a recitation?

2. Do you think tithing (giving at least 10 percent of one's net income to kingdom causes) is a biblical requirement for today's church members? A good general guideline? A legalistic, unrealistic, approach, out of line with New Testament giving? Explain.

3. Is the reading of the Law a regular part of your worship services? If not, why not? If so, why? At what point in the liturgy is it presented and in what form? What suggestions, if any, do you have for making this part of the liturgy more effective?

4. Agree or disagree: The major purpose of church education is to prepare a person to make public profession of faith.

SACRAMENTS
AND THE LITURGY

A POPULAR SINGER ONCE BAPTIZED A convert in a friend's swimming pool. The deed was not done rashly—at least not from the entertainer's point of view. He had met a desperate person. He had shown him carefully and thoroughly how Jesus Christ was the answer to his problems. He had gotten strong signs of repentance, faith, and commitment. All was done from an open Bible, with Spirit-led prayer. The celebrity was a responsible Philip to a modern Ethiopian.

But did he do right in administering a sacrament?

Sometimes Christians celebrate the Lord's Supper at retreats or conferences, outside the framework of an established congregation. Participants argue that the practice both captures and creates a strong bond of Christian unity. They testify to the meaning and effectiveness of the sacrament under such conditions, heartily recommending that other Christians try it. They claim that done intimately and informally, the supper, like early Christian meetings in Jerusalem homes, is spiritually potent.

But are such meals genuinely sacramental? Are they any different than the backyard baptism?

The backyard baptism and the retreat supper pose several sacramental questions. There are many more. For instance, why are sacraments included in worship? Do we really need them, or can we get by without them? Do they say things the Word does not? If not, why do we keep them? Do they accomplish something which the Word cannot? If so, what is it? How are sacraments related to the participants' faith? If babies and children may be baptized, may they also have the Lord's Supper? Why one but not the other? Is Christ present in the bread and the wine? Does baptism wash away sins? When, where, and by whom are sacraments to be conducted? Why? What is it that sacraments are supposed to do? Do they really do it? How many sacraments are there? Who decides? How? Are sacraments part of worship's dialogue? Are they events in which God speaks, or ceremonies in which the church acts? What is the proper way to do the sacraments?

Obviously, questions about sacraments have never been few or simple. They were the most divisive questions in the Reformation. In that movement more was written on the subject of sacraments than on any other topic. Sacramental issues separated Protestants from Rome and blocked unity among reformers. Even today the sacramental questions are among the most basic ones in ecumenical discussions. They affect both theological understanding and liturgical practice. Therefore, sacramental tastes and preferences which are dictated more by what is in cultural vogue than by what is in the Bible will not do.

SIGNS AND SEALS OF GRACE

In Reformed churches sacraments have been called "signs and seals of divine grace." They have been defined, along with preaching, as "the chief means of grace." These descriptions stress the visual and reaffirming nature of sacraments. Like

a married man who is reassured of his wife's love and fidelity by looking at his wedding band, the church's faith is strengthened by baptism and the Lord's Supper. The sacraments are displays and guarantees of God's saving love in Jesus Christ.

Sacraments, then, are essential to the church's well-being. They are dramatic, impressive, solemn pledges that God washes his peoples' sins away and nourishes them with Christ's benefits. In an era when advertisers' gospels enter our hearts through our eyes, it is imperative that the church not neglect God's sacramental means of grace.

More than two? But are there not many visual signs and seals of God's grace? Is not the cross that hangs in the chancel a confirmation of Christ's atonement for our sins? Do not the scenes on the stained glass windows assure us that God's work marched through redemptive history with authority and purpose? Are not the banners on the walls visualizations of the gospel, the height of the sanctuary a reinforcement of God's majesty and exaltedness?

The answer to these questions, of course, is yes. Yet, while all of these symbols vividly impress God's grace upon us, only those ceremonies instituted by Christ and commanded of his church qualify as sacraments. Of these there are only two—baptism and the Lord's Supper. Other ceremonies and symbols are options in worship. And the Reformed and Presbyterian traditions have been frugal in exercising those options.

Thus, after the Reformation, the sacraments were pared back from seven to two. Vestments, windows, stations of the cross, candles, incense, relics, rings, staffs, and thrones were all discarded. The pulpit and its open Bible were the dominant fixtures in worship. They were reinforced by the font and the table. Such simplicity is

a far cry from the four hundred visualizations of grace or sacraments which one early church father listed. But it supports the Reformed principle that visual simplicity is the clearest, most forceful depiction of how grace chiefly enters our lives.

"Chief" Others might ask even larger questions: Does not God confirm faith and seal grace in many ways? Why are sacraments so important? Does God not come in the counsel of a friend when our spirits are crushed? Is not the arrival of a long-prayed-for child a gracious deliverance from despair? Will God not sometimes use an illness as a warning and an instrument for repentance? Does grace, then, not employ many means? Do not all events and circumstances in life have the potential of being sacramental?

These are valid questions. The God who made and upholds all things has them at his disposal. We can never predict when or how God will shatter us with his blows or remake us in his tenderness. But these others are always secondary and derived means of grace. God's Word and his sacraments are primary. We must ask, who put counsel in the friend's mouth? Who sowed the yearning for children as one of God's greatest blessings? Who enables one to hear warning in a catastrophe? These do not come as bolts from the blue. They are shaped and prepared by years of teaching God's truth to his people and of sealing it to believers. "Chief" is an important, essential qualifier when speaking of sacraments as a means of grace.

UNION WITH CHRIST

Those who receive God's saving grace are in union with Christ. Another way of explaining sacraments, therefore, is to call them signs and seals of our union with Christ. Those joined to Christ are a body—his body—and not a random collection of individualists and free spirits. That is why sacraments belong to the church. They have been given to the body of believers to signify and

108 to seal its union with the Lord. Sacraments express and strengthen the comm-union (i.e., common union of community unity) of the saints.

The problem that Reformed believers have with baptizing a convert in a friend's swimming pool or with celebrating the supper at a retreat is that such practices make private what belongs to the entire body. For this reason, among others, they have rejected private, family baptism and brought the sacrament back into public worship. When people are united to Christ, they join his body, and that body promises to nurture and to sustain them in their union with the Lord. Moreover, each time the sacrament is administered, union with Christ is signified and sealed again to every believer present.

Similarly, as Paul teaches in 1 Corinthians 11, the Lord's Supper is not a dinner party for select guests. Even gatherings of well-intentioned believers or of worthwhile organizations ultimately inhibit Christian unity when they mimic the sacrament. The supper belongs within the ecclesiastical framework. Here the appointed, sustained, and recognized context for preaching, nurture, fellowship, and discipline in Christ's name give the supper an integral place in the ongoing life of Christ's body. Denominational Protestantism is already a creaking and splintered structure; Christian unity is only further impaired when sacraments are carried outside the life of the instituted church.

A clinching argument for identifying sacraments with the institutional church is that it is the only structure in society whose focus or primary purpose of existing is to foster union with Christ. All other structures have their distinct purposes. Families guard marriages and raise children. Schools educate. Businesses buy and sell needed goods and services at a profit. Governments promote justice. All of them do their jobs best and are a source of blessing to society when those running them do so in union with the Lord. But it is only the church whose primary calling is to call all of society to union with Christ through repentance and faith. The church should not usurp the responsibilities of other institutions, nor allow them to take over its duties. By the Word, the church brings people into union with Christ; by the sacraments, it seals that union; by healthy discipline, it protects that union. The sacraments confirm to believers that, cleansed and forgiven, they are joined to Christ.

The two Protestant sacraments, then, belong to the essence of the church. The one guarantees the birth of the church by grace. The other assures its preservation and nourishment with God's saving food and drink. Both sacraments distinguish the church as the body of believers who are in union with Christ. They mark the boundaries between the church and the world. Baptism signifies our death and burial with Christ and our being raised to new life in him. The supper is a fellowship in the body and blood of Christ.

THE PRACTICE OF BAPTISM

Christ, as Head of the church, instituted baptism when he commissioned the apostles:

> "Go therefore and make disciples of all nations, baptizing them in the name of the Father and of the Son and of the Holy Spirit, teaching them to observe all that I have commanded you; and lo, I am with you always, to the close of the age."
>
> —Matthew 28:19-20

Tied to discipline and to subsequent instruction in the faith, baptism was first practiced by Christians at Pentecost (Acts 2:38-41). It appears throughout Acts and the letters as the sacrament marking church membership. Since that time the church has continued to practice baptism as the ceremony of initiation into the people of God through the cleansing from sin.

Among the pressing questions about its practice is the matter of adult versus infant baptism. Since the New Testament does not give a direct answer to that question, debate continues. How one answers it depends on whether one sees the sacrament as a sign and seal of grace received or of grace promised; of human response, or of divine action. With a great and wide group of Christians throughout history, Reformed believers see the sacrament as a promise of God's action. Superceding circumcision, the mark of membership in the Old Testament church, baptism seals God's promises to believers and their children. The church thus baptizes infants born to believing parents.

Faithful parents Inherent in the Reformed position is the conviction that God's Spirit works through faithful parents. Parental love, instruction, counsel, and forgiveness are God's appointed ways of reaching his children with his gospel. This is not to deny that God's saving and cleansing grace is a matter of the heart, nor to claim that it is automatic. It simply explains how God reaches our hearts with his Spirit. Faithful, diligent Christian parents press the claims of Christ on their children in the conviction that God will bless their efforts to their childrens' everlasting life.

Obviously, then, children are full members of the church. They enjoy Christ's blessings, sing his praises, are reassured by his protection, often shame their elders in their witness, and bear Christian responsibilities. Children and young people have the mark of Christ on their foreheads! They are neither second-rate nor insignificant members of the body. They are full members who have simply not yet been "granted the privileges of full communion."

In this connection we must reemphasize that for baptized young adults profession of faith is not an act of joining the church. It is the public acceptance of Christian responsibilities. With that acceptance comes the invitation to sit at the Lord's table. But the Christian child has been in communion with Christ and his people from infancy. Baptism guarantees that communion from cradle to grave.

Only in the case of adult converts does profession of faith become part of the baptism ceremony. The adult testifies that the same faith is in him as Christian parents and the church nurture in their children.

How and when The important symbol in the sacrament of baptism is the water, which depicts our cleansing in Christ. Christians have used that water in many different ways: sprinkling on the forehead, effusion (pouring over the person), or total immersion. Arguments that the words *baptism* or *baptize* require one mode over another are unconvincing. Archeological excavations of the earliest churches in Asia Minor have uncovered baptistries, which indicate effusion was probably used there. These early Christians also used salt, milk, honey, oil, ritual robes, and much else in the baptism ceremony. All these details are secondary. What is indispensable is the use of the water as one is baptized in the name of the triune God.

Liturgically the sacrament of baptism follows the second Word of God in the service, the Word of assurance and forgiveness. This is the most appropriate place for the sacrament that assures us of being washed in Christ. It is also evidence that the sacraments are not bound to preaching alone, but that they portray and confirm the whole Word of God in worship.

The font should be placed prominently in the front of the sanctuary; as a visible sign and seal of

grace, the sacrament must be seen by the congregation. The custom of asking younger children to surround the font is important for the same reason, not simply because it adds informality to worship. It is also important that the congregation participate in the sacrament. Members should together take vows to support the child, accepting her as a fellow member. Then they should join the family and minister in singing a baptismal hymn of praise and thanksgiving.

Contemporary writer Seitze Buning tells a humorous story of a thirsty minister who drank from the baptismal basin. The point of the story is clear: baptism water comes from a faucet—there is no magic in it. The power is in what that water represents. When practiced in faith, the sacrament of baptism is a mighty means of grace for the entire congregation.

CELEBRATION OF THE SUPPER

Jesus instituted the Lord's Supper in the upper room the night he was betrayed.

> Now as they were eating, Jesus took bread, and blessed, and broke it, and gave it to the disciples and said, "Take, eat; this is my body." And he took a cup, and when he had given thanks he gave it to them, saying, "Drink of it, all of you; for this is my blood of the covenant, which is poured out for many for the forgiveness of sins. . . . "
>
> —Matthew 26:26–28

Mark 14:22–25, Luke 22:14–20, and 1 Corinthians 11:23–26 repeat the institution in virtually the same words. And Acts pictures the New Testament Christians breaking bread and fellowshipping together.

Paul explains the sacrament as a fellowship or communion in the body and in the blood of Christ—a communion in Christ and with fellow believers (1 Cor. 10:16). He also calls it a memorial or a witness. And then he tells us what Jesus commanded—"Do this in remembrance of me"—and he says that in celebrating the sacrament we "proclaim the Lord's death until he comes" (1 Cor. 11:25–26).

Several features emerge from the biblical material. We learn, first, that the Lord's Supper is a remembrance, a memorial meal. Second, it is also a communion or fellowship meal. Third, it is a thanksgiving celebration or eucharist. Finally, it is a witness or testimony (1 Cor. 11:26). All four features belong to the sacrament, though all have not received equal emphasis in all times or places.

The biblical words have also guided the practice of the supper. Most churches read the institution and follow Jesus' instructions for breaking the bread and pouring the wine, often to the letter. Some have even argued that Jesus required the use of one, common cup. Others emphasize the taking or the giving of the elements.

History of the Supper Evidence shows that the early Christians celebrated the sacrament weekly, on the Lord's Day, after preaching and reading the Word. The sacrament, or "liturgy of the faithful," always followed the service of the Word, or the "liturgy of the catechumens." These early worshipers often brought offerings of thanks to the eucharist—including the elements used in the sacrament.

Not until the twelfth century did transubstantiation, the position that the bread and wine become the body and blood of Christ, become official teaching. It was tied to two ideas: first, that the mass offered Christ's sacrifice anew, and second, that the church was the dispenser of divine grace.

Though the reformers largely broke with late medieval thought and practice, Calvin argued for weekly communion—unsuccessfully. New Protestants, reacting to the abuses of the Roman Catholic Church, were suspicious of the sacrament. They limited the celebration of the supper to four times a year, and they explained, in long, carefully worded forms, the correct view of the sacrament. The infrequent service of the sacrament became

the occasion for deep, thorough self-examination. As Calvin pointed out, since the supper was not automatically effective, it was important for God's people to examine their hearts and lives for proof of the true faith necessary for true celebration. For those who found it, Christ's presence at the sacrament was real. They were nourished by spiritually eating and drinking his body and blood.

New trends Many Reformed Christians today are impatient with the lengthy and somber celebration of the sacrament that has been traditional in our churches for so many years. They are eager to return to the ways of the early church; they want frequent communion services that highlight celebration and thanksgiving.

In their eagerness to change the communion liturgy, such Christians run the risk of bringing tension and anxiety to others in the congregation. Before any change in liturgy is decided on, those on both sides of the issue should become fully informed on the entire matter and should treat each other with love. The congregation should also make sure that the new liturgy adheres to the four biblical dimensions noted above.

It is also important to remember that there is no ecumenical or theological consensus on exactly what took place in the early church's celebration of the supper. That fact explains the variation in the liturgies of all those who are attempting to pattern the supper today after early church practices. But an order emerging across denominational lines usually includes the following items, more or less in the same order.

1. The Offering—during a hymn following the sermon—of money, bread and wine, brought by the deacons or others.

2. A Call to "lift up your hearts"—known as the *Sursum Corda*, and often preceded by a short statement of introduction.

3. The Thanksgiving or Eucharistic Prayer—an expression of gratitude for what God has done in Christ.

4. The *Sanctus*—praise of God's holiness, either by words spoken in unison, included in the above prayer, or by a song like "Holy, Holy, Holy."

5. The Institution—read from the Gospels or 1 Corinthians.

6. The Memorial or *Anamnesis*—a statement or affirmation to "remember Christ's death until he comes."

7. The Prayer of Consecration— includes the *epiclesis* or appeal for the Holy Spirit's presence, and may conclude with the Lord's Prayer.

8. The Communion—includes the breaking of the bread or the fraction, the blessing of the cup, the distribution of the elements, and the sacrament itself.

9. The Affirmation of Thanks and Dedication—either by a psalm, a song, or a prayer.
10. The Dismissal.

The items with technical names are among the oldest and most essential in the communion liturgy. Despite the rather lengthy list, the service above proceeds quite quickly. Many of the items occur in traditional Reformation forms for communion, as a careful comparison will demonstrate.

Reformed Christians receive the elements while seated in their pews or around tables in the chancel, seldom while kneeling. The latter posture was identified with venerating the elements as though they had become Christ's body and blood.

Bread and wine should be used if at all possible, though it is now common to substitute grape juice out of concern for alcoholic members. Liturgical scholars still dispute whether staple foods and drinks from other cultures may be substituted. Leftover elements should be disposed of respectfully, even though they are not inherently sacred. One Swiss pastor's practice of using the bread for fondue probably does not qualify. A colleague's custom of feeding it to the birds probably does.

Two thorny questions are related. Baptized children ought not be admitted to the table, since Paul's injunction to "discern the body" presupposes spiritual understanding and discrimination usually not possessed until adolescence. In the same passage Paul suggests reserving the table for faithful Christians. Thus, supervising communion and withholding it from those under discipline are good practices.

THE SACRAMENTS AS WORSHIP

Sacraments are a continuation of the worship dialogue. Though it has sometimes been said that in the sacraments God's Word and our response converge, this is true only of the acts of sprinkling, eating, and drinking. In all other parts of the sacraments God's Word and the congregation's responses are distinguishable. But in the sacramental actions per se there is both a divine giving and a believing reception. God gives his seals or confirmed promises of grace, and the church receives the signs in faith. In these three actions there is a holy intimacy between God and his people.

In celebrating the sacraments, therefore, Christians worship God. By observing the ceremonies Christ instituted, they render God his rightful service (liturgy) and acknowledge his worthiness (worship).

A. PERSONAL QUESTIONS/COMMENTS ON
CHAPTER 9

B. Reflecting on the "Last Supper"

Read Matthew 26:17–30

Imagine that you were present with Jesus and the other disciples at the Last Supper. Spend a few minutes by yourself quietly thinking about this. What was it like? How did you feel toward your fellow disciples? Toward your Lord? What impact did Jesus' words about his body and blood have on you?

This is not an exegetical exercise in which you try to understand the text. That too is important, but not for this exercise. This exercise is meant to help you "experience" the text as though it were happening to you.

Meditate for five minutes or so. Then be ready to share your reactions with others.

C. Participating in the Lord's Supper Today

Discuss your experiences at the Lord's Supper. What do you think/feel about your fellow believers? About Jesus Christ? Do you expect and receive some kind of "emotional lift" from the supper? Should you?

D. Discussing Issues Related to the Lord's Supper

1. Should twelve-year-old children who've given some evidence of genuine faith be allowed to participate in the Lord's Supper?

    Of course, the Bible doesn't directly answer this question. However it's covenant theme clearly indicates that children of believers are full members of the body of Christ. For that reason they are baptized and for that reason, some argue, they should be allowed to participate in the supper. To deny them this is to apply the covenant theme in one place but not in the other. Additional biblical evidence is found in Exodus 12, where young children obviously participated in the rite of Passover.

    Although children don't know the details of the Reformed faith, they do know enough, presumably, to avoid "unworthy partaking," as described in 1 Corinthians 11. And who will deny that children's faith can be real? As one Canadian writer puts it, "They can be (and so often are) children of God who in their own way have knowledge of sin and rejoice in salvation through Christ and struggle to lead a Christian life. Their faith needs strengthening too, just as much as the faith of their parents." Proponents also note that the major religious traditions (Lutheran, Anglican, Catholic, for example) allow for early participation of children in the sacrament. Calvin himself said that a ten-year-old who knew the Creed, the Commandments, the Lord's Prayer, and the Lord's Days on the sacraments was ready for communion.

    Well, that's one side of the issue, prescribed here to spark discussion. If you agree with the above, perhaps you can offer some practical suggestions for implementing the participation of children in the supper. If you don't agree with the above, what reasons, biblical and otherwise, can you cite?

    Where do you stand on the basic issue, as stated at the beginning of this question?

2. Should we restore the practice of weekly communion? How would this affect attitudes toward preaching? Could the sacrament be incorporated smoothly into each worship service? Would it become routine?

    A review of chapter 9 will turn up a number of reasons for restoring the practice of weekly communion. However, author De Jong comments (elsewhere) that this is not an issue easily resolved with immediate, dogmatic answers. De Jong hopes the issue will be thoroughly aired and carefully studied by all concerned, with the four purposes of communion firmly in mind.

    What do you think? Should the church again practice weekly communion? Review the pros and cons.

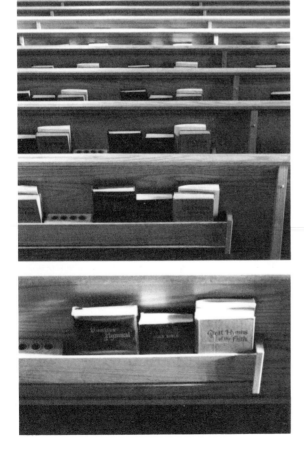

THE LITURGY
AND LIFE

I N *SURPRISED BY JOY*, HIS AUTOBIOGRAPHI-
cal account of coming to the Christian
faith, C. S. Lewis reflects on his first impressions of churchgoing. Having sorted
through many philosophies and religions, and
having concluded that Christianity offered the
best form of Theism, he was constrained by con-
sistency to attend worship services. While he generally liked the Anglican clergymen he met,
Lewis confesses, "I had as little wish to be in the
Church as in the zoo." He continues with a de-
lightfully honest description.

> It was, to begin with, a kind of collective; a
> wearisome "get-together" affair. I couldn't yet
> see how a concern of that sort should have
> anything to do with one's spiritual life. To me,
> religion ought to have been a matter of good
> men praying alone and meeting by twos and
> threes to talk of spiritual matters. And then the
> fussy, time-wasting botheration of it all! The
> bells, the crowds, the umbrellas, the notices,
> the bustle, the perpetual arranging and organ-
> izing.

He summarizes, "Thus my churchgoing was a
merely symbolical and provisional practice"
(quotes from page 187).

Obviously, at this point in his life, churchgoing
had not yet become worship for C. S. Lewis. Much
less had the services become an integral part of

his whole spiritual life and well-being. What went on in the church building on Sunday seemed to him completely unrelated to and unnecessary for the rest of his life.

Many would agree with that sentiment. Many who call themselves Christians argue that church attendance is not a necessary part of Christian living. That attitude raises an interesting question: What is the relation of worship to life?

THE GLOBAL SANCTUARY

The word *sanctuary* as a designation for a holy place more sacred than other locations does not technically belong in the Reformed vocabulary. We apply it to the big room where God and his people meet on Sundays, of course. But in our New Testament era the whole world is a sanctuary. It is consecrated ground by virtue of Christ's finished work. He has been pronounced Lord of all creation, and his redemptive power is at work in all that God has made. While the effects of his dominion are not yet fully apparent, all that exists belongs to him.

If Moses took his shoes off when he entered holy ground, the Christian church ought, in a manner of speaking, to live barefoot! The prophet Zechariah had visions of the day of the Lord, when all the world would be consecrated to him.

> And the Lord will become king over all the earth; on that day the Lord will be one and his name one . . . .
> And on that day there shall be inscribed on the bells of the horses, "Holy to the Lord." And the pots in the house of the Lord shall be as the bowls before the altar; and every pot in Jerusalem and Judah shall be sacred to the Lord of hosts, so that all who sacrifice may come and take of them and boil the flesh of the sacrifice in them. And there shall no longer be a trader in the house of the Lord of hosts on that day.
>
> —Zechariah 14:9, 20–21

Zechariah is telling us that the terrain outside the temple is as devoted to God as are the rituals within it. Not just the priest, but all the people share the sacrificial meat, the benefits of the Great Sacrifice. Even the containers for those blessings are holy.

Those living by the light of the prophet's vision today should recognize that jet travel and mass transit, gourmet dining and international grain deals belong to the Lord. They are under his dominion and must conform to his will. Life is sacred, and all of it is called to reflect the power and the glory of God's kingdom.

That Zechariah was reaffirming God's original intentions is obvious from the opening chapters of Genesis. God commanded man and woman to "Be fruitful and multiply, and fill the earth and subdue it; and have dominion . . . " (Gen. 1:28). In the next chapter God told the man and the woman to till the garden, to maintain it, and to name the animals. All of their activities were responses to God. Their faithful acts acknowledged God's worth, and hence were a form of worship. Their disobedience was an affront to God—blasphemy and idolatry; it denied his worthiness of their loyalty.

In Reformation thought every believer is a priest. He or she approaches God directly through Christ, without being held hostage to the church and its offices. A Calvinist corollary of the priesthood of all believers is the doctrine that life's occupation is a sacred calling. It too is worship which the believer brings to God. In his *Institutes of the Christian Religion*, Calvin argues that responding to God's call in our daily responsibilities is the basis for a good, wholesome, and integrated life. Furthermore, such response renders life holy and noble:

> From this will arise also a singular consolation: that no task will be so sordid and base, provided you obey your calling in it, that it will not shine and be reckoned very precious in God's sight.
>
> —III/10/vi; vol I, p. 725, McNeill ed.

Calvin, then, saw life in the same comprehensively sacred way as did the apostle Paul, who said, "So, whether you eat or drink, or whatever you do, do all to the glory of God" (1 Cor. 10:31). For both these men life was religious and the world a sanctuary.

To call only some occupations "kingdom work," therefore, is not consistent with either the Bible or the best thought in the Reformed heritage. The only tenable position is that all work done in faith and in obedience to God is worship.

LIVING THE LITURGY

We should not conclude from this that we can dispense with churches and preachers. Sacraments and sermons have not become obsolete. Christianity has not, as a modern current of theological opinion says, become "religionless" after the death and resurrection of Christ. Quite the opposite is true. The Christian worship service clarifies the meaning and reinforces the purpose of our existence.

Another way of explaining this is to say that we must live the liturgy. What we do in worship echoes and reverberates through all the activities and responsibilities of the Christian during the week. The themes of the service are amplified and varied in the symphony of our whole life. A holy harmony exists, then, between the public, official worship of God's gathered people and the work of families and individuals in their everyday praise.

A walk through the liturgy should illustrate this point.

God's greeting on Sunday morning teaches us to hear him addressing us throughout the week. His grace, mercy, and peace are spoken to us without words, in the spirit of Psalm 19. When the TV anchorman announces the ceasefire to a particularly bloody, victimizing conflict, God's grace salutes us. When we narrowly miss a kitchen accident, he greets us with his mercy. He speaks his peace in the birds' evening song. But it is the liturgy that has conditioned us to hear these continuous greetings from our heavenly Father.

Praise, thanks, and adoration are genuine only when they are dispositions of life. To "give the Lord wholehearted praise" in the opening anthem on Sunday, and then to curse the work and the responsibilities he has assigned us during the week is to take God for a fool and to make liars of ourselves. Such praise will not get past the ceiling, and the curse will backlash on the worship services. On the other hand, the woman who is grateful for her jobs, including the one at home, and the man who thankfully accepts his children and his duties toward them can sing heartily in church.

We must live our religion!

Because we never consistently do, life, like the liturgy, must contain times of genuine contrition and penitence. And real penitence is more than words. If we are genuinely sorry for misrepresenting a product in the salesroom, we not only vow to change our "pitch," but we call the bamboozled customer and tell him the truth. James told us, "Confess your sins to one another" (James 5:16). The closer and more intently we live with others, the more crucial his instruction becomes. The depth and quality of our relationships is directly proportional to our willingness to confess wrongs and to accept forgiveness.

Living our religion is hard! That is why God speaks his Word of grace and forgiveness. Spoken from the pulpit, read in the Bible, it is transmitted through a mother's arms around a rowdy child who has just broken a piece of china. It comes through the words of a counselor who has brought an alienated couple through a period of reconciliation. It is conveyed in the clasped hands of long-hostile brothers. The week is not long enough to contain the reconciliation and assurance needed in our lives. But the ministry of reconciliation, begun by Paul in his apostolic message (2 Cor. 5:18–19), is continued by all believers in their lives with others (Matt. 5:24).

Through the liturgy God shapes us to live expectantly. The Christian life is a life of great anticipations. They rest on God's promises. They are expressed in our prayers for help and divine blessing. Looking for God's provision and assistance from one day to the next, whether we are scanning the sky for rain clouds or the want ads for work, becomes a spiritual reflex for believers. As we live and breathe, we pray.

We also listen. We hear God's counsel, warnings, encouragements, and instruction in inner-city social conditions and in political developments in Ottawa or Washington. While we may never be spooked by "divine providences" as the Puritans often were, we must discern the signs of our times. The word preached on Sunday illumines and interprets the news on Thursday. Reinhold Niebuhr's advice to his students is good for all Christians: "Your two indispensable sources for understanding the world must be the Bible and the *New York Times*." Always in that order!

The liturgy might as well be chiseled in granite if its dedication and commitment do not take on the warmth and flesh of our lives. The author of Hebrews says,

> Through him then let us continually offer up the sacrifice of praise to God, that is, the fruit of lips that acknowledge his name. Do not neglect to do good and to share what you have, for such sacrifices are pleasing to God
> —Hebrews 13:15–16

Whether it is in an offering, in our confession of the creed, in our public vows, or in a prayer—sung or spoken—our affirmation of service to God and others is on the line all week.

The liturgy, then, is not ritual magic which works a protective spell over our existence. It is the sum and substance of our lives. It is the presentation of ourselves to the Lord for his benediction. It is also the pattern by which we cut the cloth of our experiences. Another way of putting it, turning things just around, is to say that life is the incarnation of the liturgy.

To be genuine worship, the liturgy must be lived.

LIFE AS DIALOGUE

Throughout our study of worship and liturgy we have consistently called the worship service a dialogue between God and his people. Dialogue is the best and the basic description of what occurs in worship.

The appropriateness of this description is based on the covenental understanding of biblical religion. The faith of the Bible is the believers' response to God's revelation. It belongs to a relationship between two people capable of communicating with one another. From the time God came down to the garden and spent the evening communicating with Adam and Eve, God has addressed his people and they have responded to him.

The nature of the communication between God and his people is gracious. It's content is commitment. God obligates himself to his people in his promises. The people are bound to him by the terms which he defines and they accept. The biblical word for this two-way commitment, this bond with obligations on both sides, is *covenant*. The relationship between God and his people, then, is a covenantal relationship.

Covenantal commitment was never limited to what our culture narrowly calls "religion." To be sure, in the Old Testament specifications were given for sacrifices, the tabernacle and temple, the priesthood and Levites, feasts, and sabbaths. But covenant duties were also specified for marriage, raising a family, political policy, agriculture, and commerce.

The same holds true of our covenantal relationship today. Our daily lives speak volumes about the health and integrity of our relationship with God. Often we say more to him and to others by our actions than by our words.

The dialogical character of worship, then, is part of the dialogical character of our entire existence. The dialogue must be faithful to the covenant design of our relationship with God. To say that life is a covenant dialogue is to give biblical and theological footing to the affirmation that we are called to live the liturgy.

No Foggy Lenses

The gift of Christian worship is God's way of keeping our life focused on Christ. When we neglect the means of grace, the meaning of our existence becomes fogged over like a pair of cloudy glasses. Where worship is shaped by biblically faithful liturgical guidelines, and is attended regularly by God's people, they will generally be able to pick their way through life with clarity and discernment. They will usually be able to keep their spiritual eyes on the Lord.

The relatedness of life and liturgy add significance to liturgical issues and discussions. When liturgical changes are proposed, people sense that something basic to their identity and to their way of life is at stake. Sometimes both those who want change and those who resist it react more with their viscera than with their heads. But intuitively all concerned know three things. They know that their faith is expressed in liturgy. They understand that liturgical changes will affect the expression of their faith. They sense that some-

how their lives, or at least their understanding of them, will be tempered by modifying the worship service.

When liturgical change is borrowed indiscriminately from many sources, it may contribute to confusion of the church's faith and the compromise of its life. Liturgical conservatism may be no more helpful, as it may produce a church that worships more by ritual than by faith and whose existence in the modern world is not directed one whit by the obsolete practices used in worship.

Yet people on both sides can make a significant contribution to the liturgy. They can clarify the church's faith by contributing to proper liturgy. They can also impart a sense of direction in life.

Since the church is a living organism in a changing world, creative and fresh approaches to worship are in order. Since it is a body that lives by a confession and that has continuity with the past, durable and proven patterns ought not to be discarded. They give the church identity and unity.

Where the liturgy is valued, the likelihood of keeping faith and life in focus is great. As outlined and explained in this study, the basic structure of Reformed liturgy has been tested by the four essential principles. It has the common features of all Christian worship; hence it is catholic. It is founded on God's Word; thus it is biblical. It is shaped by the features of the Reformed faith; therefore it is confessional. It encourages sensitivity to local needs and tastes; hence it is pastoral.

When the structure of the liturgy provides the pattern for sensitive creative worship, the likelihood is great that the church will live its liturgy. In such a setting, it will also discover that its liturgy lives for it.

A. Personal Questions/Comments on
Chapter 10

1. Review (and add to) the ways that the various parts of the liturgy can be expressed in our day-to-day lives. Which liturgical items seem to transfer themselves rather naturally into our lives? Which seem more difficult to incorporate into the way we live?

2. In your opinion does your congregation tend to resist liturgical change or welcome it? In other words, is your congregation liturgically conservative or liturgically innovative? Give examples, if possible. After reaching a consensus (or a truce), discuss the degree to which your congregation studies and understands its liturgical posture.

1. From your study and reading, what principles for Reformed worship would you describe as nonnegotiable, or absolutely essential? List as many such principles as you can.

2. Dr. De Jong began this course by defining Reformed worship as "a prescribed, corporate meeting between God and his people, in which God is praised and his church is blessed." Having studied the various aspects of worship for some ten sessions now, do you agree with the definition? Would you want to modify it in some way?

3. We hope the course has been useful to you. Perhaps group members could comment briefly on the book and on the group sessions. What has been most beneficial/helpful/useful/ interesting to you personally? What could stand improvement?

Alexander, David and Patricia, eds. *Eerdmans' Handbook to the Bible*. William B. Eerdmans Publishing Co., 1983

The Banner. November 24, 1980 and May 31, 1982.

Benton, F. F. *Music in the Christian Reformed Church: Its Calvinistic, Systematic Theological Influences and Its Development since 1857*. Master's thesis, Mankato State University, 1975.

Berkhof, Louis. *Systematic Theology*. Grand Rapids, Mich.: William B. Eerdmans Publishing Co., 1949.

Berkouwer, G. C. *The Sacraments*. Grand Rapids, Mich.: William B. Eerdmans Publishing Co., 1969.

Bromiley, G. W., ed. *The International Standard Bible Encyclopedia*. Grand Rapids, Mich.: William B. Eerdmans Publishing Co., 1979.

Bruce, F. F. "The Speeches of Acts." In *The Acts of the Apostles*. Grand Rapids: William B. Eerdmans Publishing Co., 1951.

Bruggink, Donald and Carl Coppers. *Christ and Architecture*. Grand Rapids, Mich. : William B. Eerdmans Publishing Co., 1965.

Bushell, Michael. *Songs of Zion*. Pittsburgh: Crown and Covenant Publications, 1980.

Calvin, John. *Institutes of the Christian Religion*. Translated by Henry Beveridge. Grand Rapids, Mich.: William B. Eerdmans Publishing Co., 1953.

Daane, James. *Preaching with Confidence: A Theological Essay on the Power of the Pulpit*. Grand Rapids, Mich.: William B. Eerdmans Publishing Co., 1980.

Duckworth, Robert, ed. *This Is the Word of the Lord: Year A, the Year of Matthew*. New York: Oxford University Press, 1980.

_____. *This Is the Word of the Lord: Year B, the Year of Mark*. New York: Oxford University Press, 1981.

_____. *This Is the Word of the Lord: Year C, the Year of Luke*. New York: Oxford University Press, 1982.

Davies, J. G., ed. *The Westminster Dictionary of Worship*. Philadelphia: The Westminster Press, 1972.

"Dance and the Christian Life." In *Acts of Synod*, 1982, 556-575. Grand Rapids, Mich.: Christian Reformed Board of Publications, 1982.

Douglas, J. D., ed. *The New Bible Dictionary*. Grand Rapids, Mich. William B. Eerdmans Publishing Co., 1962.

Engle, Paul. *Discovering the Fullness of Worship*. Philadelphia: Great Commission Publications, 1978.

Hageman, Howard. "The Liturgical Origins of the Reformed Churches." In *The Heritage of John Calvin*, 110-136. Edited by John H. Bratt. Grand Rapids, Mich.: William B. Eerdmans Publishing Co., 1973.

_____. *Pulpit and Table*. Richmond: John Knox Press, 1962.

Heyns, William. *Liturgiek*. Holland, Mich.: Holkeboer, 1903.

Hoekema, Anthony. "Theological Criteria for a Good Hymn." *The Banner*, January 19, 1981.

Liturgy and Music in Reformed Worship. Louisville: The Joint Office of Worship of the Presbyterian Church (USA). Published quarterly.

Jones, Wainwright, and Yarnold, eds. *The Study of Liturgy*. New York: Oxford University Press, 1978.

128

Lewis, Clive Staples. *Letters to Malcolm: Chiefly on Prayer*. London and Glasgow: Collins, Fontana Books, 1964.

_____. *Surprised by Joy*. London and Glasgow: Collins, Fontana Books, 1955.

Lyles, Jean Caffey. "To Animate the Body of Christ: Sarah Bentley Talks about Sacred Dance." In *The Christian Century*, May 19, 1982, 601-605.

Macleod, Donald I. "Meaning in Worship." In *Presbyterian Worship* (revised edition), 1-20. Atlanta: John Knox Press, 1980.

Martin, Ralph P. *Worship in the Early Church*. Grand Rapids, Mich.: William B. Eerdmans Publishing Co., 1974.

Marshall, I. H. "Luke's Theological Motivation: the Speeches of Acts." In *The Acts of the Apostles, Tyndale New Testament Commentaries*, Vol. 5. Grand Rapids, Mich.: William B. Eerdmans Publishing Co., 1980.

Maxwell, William D. *An Outline of Christian Worship*. London: Oxford University Press, 1936.

Proceedings: A Conference on Liturgy and Music in Reformed Worship. Grand Rapids, Mich.: Board of Publications of the Christian Reformed Church, 1979.

Polman, Bert F. *Church Music and Liturgy in the Christian Reformed Church of North America*. Ph.D diss., University of Minnesota, 1980.

Rayburn, Robert G. *O Come, Let Us Worship: Corporate Worship in the Evangelical Church*. Grand Rapids, Mich.: Baker Book House, 1980.

"Report of the Liturgical Committee." In *Acts of Synod*, 1968. Grand Rapids, Mich: Board of Publications of the Christian Reformed Church, 1968.

Thompson, Bard, ed. *Liturgies of the Western Church*. New York: World Publishing Co., Meridian, 1967.

Von Allmen, J. J. *Worship: Its Theology and Practice*. New York: Oxford University Press, 1966.

Wainright, Geoffrey. *Doxology: The Praise of God in Worship, Doctrine, and Life*. New York: Oxford University Press, 1980.

Westerman, Claus. *Blessing in the Bible and the Life of the Church*. Philadelphia: Fortress Press, 1978.